Grief's Liturgy

Grief's Liturgy

A Lament

Gerald J. Postema

WIPF & STOCK · Eugene, Oregon

GRIEF'S LITURGY
A Lament

Wipf & Stock
An Imprint of Wipf and Stock Publishers
199 W. 8th Ave., Suite 3
Eugene, OR 97401
www.wipfandstock.com

ISBN 13: 978-1-61097-182-9
Manufactured in the U.S.A.

Contents

List of Illustrations

Preface

LINDA DIED A LITTLE more than a year ago. I gathered into this lament some of the thoughts, images, poetry, and music that sat with me like gentle good friends as I grieved. I call it "grief's liturgy," relying on the original Greek meaning of the word *liturgy*— the work of the people, which, of course, is commonly associated with the people's work of worship. There is, perhaps, an element of worship in this lament, but the emphasis is on work. The following pages give expression to a year's hard work of grieving. It is a record of one person's grieving. But over the course of the year I have gradually come to learn that no matter how isolated I felt, I was never truly alone in my grief. It takes a community to grieve the loss of a loved one, and the community of people who loved Linda grieved with me. So, in a way, "grief's liturgy" is the record of a people's work of grieving seen through the experience of a person at its center.

This grief is expressed as a lament, rather than as a chronicle or narrative. This lament may share something with the expressive nature of a threnody (hymn of mourning), but it is, I fear, less refined and carefully constructed than that characterization might suggest. These pages record the sighs, shrieks, songs, and prayers nearly as they occurred, accompanied by reflections on them, on the events and experiences that prompted them, and on the poetry, prose, and paintings that accompanied me through the year. If it had been possible, I would have also included music, for often music carried me from one moment to the next when nothing else could. But in the place of music, you will, from time to time, run across portions of text that might be sung or accompanied by a performance of associated music.

I have structured the following readings, reflections, and remembrances roughly on the model of the liturgy of hours (the Christian Divine Office), in cycles of *lauds* (dawn), *terce* (mid-morning), *sext* (noon), *none* (afternoon), *vespers* (early evening), *compline* (late evening, the close of the day), and *vigil* (night). Occasionally, *terce*, *sext*, and *none* are folded into "Daytime." The liturgy of the hours prescribes that each "hour" begin with Psalm 70:1 (69: 2)—"Be pleased, O God, to deliver me; Lord make haste to help me!" It is a fitting preamble for these reflections, and the careful reader may "hear" this invocation intoned at the opening of each section. Each hour has its own feel or tone, or so it seems to me. Accordingly, I have associated each hour not with a time of day but rather with a theme, focus, or emotional tone, much like the tone composers associate with musical keys. I associate *vigil* with darkness, silence, solitude, and anxious keeping watch for the morning; *lauds* with daybreak and renewed promise; *terce* with movement into the light of day in the presence of others and doing the work of love; *sext* with elegy and celebration; *none* with lessons learned from the experience of the day; *vespers* with twilight's between-times and so with reflection, and sometimes a sense of my beloved's presence; and finally, *compline* with comfort, but also anxiety for what the night brings, and, so, with commending one's soul to divine safekeeping. *Compline* is followed again, of course, by *vigil* and its sometimes terrifying night thoughts.

The designations at the beginning of each entry alert the reader to the tone or mood of the entry to follow. But the order of the "hours" is not rigidly followed, as is fitting for the irregular movement of grief. Likewise, the designated themes of the entries are meant to be only rough suggestions and are not meant to exclude other possibilities. The "days" offer a cycle of such themes and tones, building on and sometimes referring to previous "days" and "hours," but not proceeding as an unfolding progression. Lament is characterized more by juxtaposition than linear movement; so sudden, sharp changes of mood or thought and even inconsistency are inevitable.

I wish to express my gratitude to the Duke Institute on Care at the End of Life for its generous support of this project and to Brett McCarty for help in preparing this work for publication.

August 13, 2009
Ordinary Time
Chapel Hill, North Carolina

Introit

Introit I

Email Message: Wednesday, May 14, 2008

Dear Friends,

Linda, the love, joy, and very center of my life, died last night. When we learned Monday that no further chemotherapy options were likely to prove beneficial and that Linda probably did not have the physical resources to cope with their expected side-effects, we engaged hospice services to help ease her pain and difficult breathing. Hospice nurses arrived at our home and began their ministrations late afternoon Tuesday. A few hours later, she died.

At the time of her death, we were surrounded by friends.

Jerry

For nearly two and a half years Linda worked with formidable determination to deny lung cancer control of her life; when the time came, she denied it control of her death. In her final hours, her pain was overwhelming; her struggle with the evil inside her was terrible. But when the pain released its grip, she chose to let go. Linda—not the cancer—said, "It is finished." I was there. I held her hand. I whispered my love. Gradually she became very quiet. I sat with her. I leaned close to kiss her. No breath!

Grief's Liturgy

God take her! Wrap her in your arms!
May the eternal light of your steadfast love surround her.
Lux aeterna luceat eis, Domine.

Sleep, O sleep in the calm of each calm.
Sleep, O sleep in the guidance of all guidance.
 Sleep, O sleep in the love of all loves.
 Sleep, O beloved, in the Lord of life.
 Sleep, O beloved, in the God of life.

     —THE EBBA COMPLINE

Introit II

I heard a voice say, "Cry!"
I said: "What shall I cry?"

—Isaiah 40:6 (NIV)

"We are summoned to a silent place," John Bell wrote, "struggling to find some words to fill the space." But why must we look for words to fill the space? Isn't silence better? Is anything but silence possible?

In his "Requiem for a Friend," Rilke looked for words to "set it all in order." But I wonder what is one to set in order? Death? There is nothing orderly about death; and to make death into something orderly, to domesticate the demonic, is to deny its awful negation of all that is good. Grief, then? Grief is chaos; to set it in order is to try to capture fog with a sieve.

Still, could we not hope, perhaps, to wrest some meaning from death and grief, some why or wherefore—to grasp somehow the terrible mystery of death? But often I can only believe, with Wolterstorff, that "such shattering of love [is] beyond meaning for us, [for death is] the breaking of meaning." So, the question persists: why? Why words? Why not just allow silence to bind up the pain?

Very often, surely, silence—the aching, silent cry—is all one can manage. Even so, sometimes I found myself seeking out words, or music, or images . . . *something* to give shape to the grief, even if anything I sought was likely to be inadequate. Might there be some reason to seek out words?

Perhaps, *to name.* So much of grief is beyond, or beneath, words; ineffable sighs and cries, and pain too deep for words. But, still, we can strive to bring the ineffable, the fleeting, and the chaotic into the human melody of living and loving. Not to deny the demonic awfulness of death, but to deny its claim to dominion.

Perhaps, *to honor.* Although the why of suffering and death may always elude our grasp, we can try to capture, preserve, and honor the dying, honor a life lived in the face of death, and honor the love that lives on in the grip of grief.

Especially, *to remember.* We can seek to gather the fragments of love left scattered by the demands of living with illness, to reassemble them and breathe renewed life into them. This remembering is a sacred, sacramental work of love.

Perhaps, through the work of naming, honoring, and remembering, we may be permitted to touch that which is beyond touch, to enter the garden of what T. S. Eliot called "this intersection time."

Introit III

Does this grieving have a name?

I cannot think of it merely as a process, something to undergo, something that happens to one. I find it even harder to think of it as a process of healing, because grieving is not pathological, although it often brings pathology in its wake. Its cause, rooted in the lifeblood of love, is the most profound treasure of the soul. In the midst of grief, to think of grief's pain as pathology is impossible. Neither can I think of grieving as a journey. The problem is not merely that we are inclined to call nearly every life process a "journey," trivializing the term. The problem is that grief is not an adventure. It is not orderly. There are no maps to guide; it has no known destination, no promise of relief or joy upon arrival. So, again, I am left wondering what is grieving's name?

In Luther's text, the familiar phrase "blessed are those who mourn" (Matthew 5:4) is rendered, "*Selig sind, die da Leid tragen*"—"blessed are those who bear grief." "Bear grief"—that seems right.

Grief is a leaden burden borne on the backs of the living,
    bending the bearer unbearably.
Grief is *liturgy*—
    extreme, exhausting, endless labor;
    sacred labor: labor set apart, singular, and profound,
        soul-engaged, soul-challenging,
        assigned and prescribed, like the divine office,
        yet unlike it because it is without a script;
To grieve the death of one's beloved is to live a lament-psalm;
    to live, weeping, a contradiction-filled, pain-racked,
        musical prayer.
Like a lament-psalm, grieving mixes guilt and grace;
    anguish and anger give way suddenly to alleluia;
    and alleluia, in a moment, sinks back into sickness of heart.

Grief's Liturgy

Occasionally, disorientation modulates to a key of reorientation—
the wounds remain, the pain still stabs, but sometimes
renewed life, scarred and broken joy, seem possible.
Yet the reorientation is momentary—never once and for all:
no feeling is final, no insight stable,
no steps forward without stumbles back,
no relief without relapse;
Grief's liturgy moves irregularly, in zig-zag patterns.

Day I

Day I: Dawn [Lauds]

I have always known
That at last I would
Take this road, but yesterday
I did not know that it would be today.

—ARIWARA NO NARIHIRA

Linda, because you departed so suddenly—at least it seemed sudden to me and to your friends who gathered around you that night—you have left to me the task of gathering and reassembling the fragments of our love. Not because our love was broken, although it needed some tender maintenance, and not because it had been neglected, although at times lately we tended to it only as background to other pressing tasks. Rather, the work of gathering must be done now because this love was so rich and generous, so joyous and fruitful, that it scattered seeds liberally and carelessly and now the flowers are growing everywhere. The gathering itself is one of those flowers—love binding up love, love binding together love in the hope of bringing forth love.

I am inadequate to the task, Darling, but I jealously keep it for myself. No one can, no one will, gather our love with as much right or as much care as I shall. Gathering and binding

Grief's Liturgy

these scattered seeds of our love, not for display on a shelf as a
work well done, but as a wondrous living thing that will continue
to grow in startling new ways as the years unfold.

My dearworthy darling,
stay close.
I need your hands
to help me gather
and your breath
to inspire.

Day I: Daytime (1)

Even youths will faint and be weary,
and the young will fall exhausted;
but those who wait for the Lord shall renew their strength,
they shall mount up with wings like eagles,
they shall run and not be weary,
they shall walk and not faint.

—ISAIAH 40: 30–31 (NRSV)

Linda and I read these words on the morning of that day in late January, 2006, when we met with her oncologist to begin her first clinical trial. It was a regime that brought her life back to nearly normal for several months. We were full of fearful apprehensiveness and uncertainty that Monday morning, but already, even then, Linda's strength was evident. Her determination to face the reality of her new life directly and with courage could be seen in her eyes. It was a difficult task for her. Yet, for two years her courage, clear-eyed realism, and gentle grace never faltered.

I wish I had her by my side now, helping me through this new trial. I fear I have neither her strength nor her courage. Worse, I don't have her calming words, her soft and caring touch, and her gentle eyes to sustain me. And sometimes . . . sometimes, the pain is more than I can bear.

Day I: Mid-Morning [Terce]

For love is as strong as death ...

—SONG OF SONGS 8:6 (NIV)

Linda died just two weeks before our thirty-ninth wedding anniversary. We were married on Memorial Day weekend, 1969. We were just kids, not yet 21 years old. Our story began nearly five years before that, in November of 1964, when Linda asked me out for our first date. Actually, if legend is to be believed, the first sparks of our love may have been struck long before that when we were kindergarten classmates. You see, Linda and I did not fall in love; it did not just happen. Love was prepared for us; it prepared us and nurtured us. In its embrace we matured into adults, and as we matured, the embrace grew stronger, the roots struck deeper. Our love was tested—by shattering disappointments, by long periods of physical separation, by thoughtless and long-regretted wounds—but it proved stronger for the testing, deeper for the challenge. Our rich, shared, and mutually treasured history and the love it nourished has extraordinary tensile strength. Stronger than death.

Day I: Noon [Sext]

Loud as a trumpet
in the vanguard of an army,
I will run ahead and proclaim.

—RILKE

Linda reacted to talk of her courage with a wry smile, not believing a word of it. Friends called it extraordinary courage, but she insisted it was nothing more than facing reality. "It's not courage. When something like this happens, you just call it what it is, and deal with it."

The truly courageous may not be the best detectors of courage.

Linda would not be comfortable with elegy. She hated embellishment. "Just tell the story, Jerry," she would so often say. "Leave out all the extra stuff and get to the point." She preferred the light of the sun to the glow of sentiment.

I, on the other hand . . .

I want to paint her in brilliant colors "in one broad sweep across heaven."

Day I: Daytime (2)

Diary entry: Friday, July 11, 2008

I have been feeling especially vulnerable and at sea this week. For most of the day on Monday I experienced abdominal pain, and in the evening I discovered I was bleeding from my gut. Disoriented and alarmed, I drove myself to the emergency room. A series of tests administered through the night showed that nothing was seriously wrong. I was discharged Tuesday, armed with antibiotics to fight the invading infection. The bleeding had shocked me, but what knocked the pins from under me was the realization that for the first time since I was a teenager Linda was not by my side, calmly assessing the situation and focusing on what needed to be done. Like an earthquake victim, I felt that something absolutely solid, a point of reference for everything else in my experience, was no longer there.

Day I: Afternoon [None]

John of Damascus wondered whether any pleasure in life is unmixed with sorrow. Grief asks whether sorrow will ever again permit pleasure into the mix.

Diary entry: August 2, 2008—7:20 a.m.

I sit here in the airport waiting for the departure of my flight to Chicago. Today I begin a ten-day trip via air, train, and automobile to Chicago, Seattle, Vancouver, and back to Chicago. It is the first vacation trip I can remember without Linda. I feel apprehensive and not a little fearful. Can this trip hold any pleasure for me? How could there be pleasure if it cannot be shared with her? Can I bear for ten days the heavy burden of emptiness I carry? At home I could lean on friends if my emotional skies turned dark. And I had my work to distract me. Yet, I don't want to be distracted. I'm living a paradox: I want to find a way of living without Linda that is not living without her. When at work, I live without her. That's the last thing I want.

My hope is that this time away from work will give me an opportunity to think about what is ahead for me, about how to live into the future. I am entirely at sea about that future. With Linda gone I scarcely know who I am. I feel like an adolescent again, with one major difference. As an adolescent I didn't know what to do with my life, with my future, but I never doubted that there was a future for me. The future was there, a vessel to be filled, though I knew not how. Second adolescence comes with no such assurance. I am not sure there is a future for me, or at least I am not sure whether there is one worth filling. Life without Linda is grim, colorless, and painful. Why live with this? Can I find something that moves me again? I do not know adult life without her. I have no adult memory that is not filled with her presence. Life, perhaps, can go on without her; but can my life go on?

Grief's Liturgy

[Sung]

> Lord help us to gather our strength in difficult times
> So that we could go on living
> Believing in the meaning of future days.

—Zbigniew Preisner

Day I: Twilight [Vespers]

C. S. Lewis writes:

> Bereavement is a universal and integral part of our ex-
> perience of love. . . . It is not a truncation of the process
> but one of its phases; not the interruption of the dance,
> but the next figure. We are "taken out of ourselves" by the
> loved one while she is here. Then comes the tragic figure
> of the dance in which we must learn to be still taken out
> of ourselves though the bodily presence is withdrawn.

I cannot accept that our dance has not been truncated. It has. We were in *mid-stride*. We were just about getting it right. Sometimes we were really spectacular—dancing with the stars. Sometimes we were pedestrian—inconsistent, but showing promise. We just needed a little more practice.

Still, Lewis does hit the right note at the end of this passage when he writes, "to love the very Her, and not to fall back to loving our past, or our memory, or our sorrow, or our relief from sorrow, or our own love." That's the great difficulty, I believe, and my great fear. In this new phase of our dance of love, how am I to love Linda, *the very her*, and not my memory of her, or some fiction I have created of her? Loving the beloved who has died, Lewis observes, is like loving God:

> The earthly beloved, even in this life, incessantly tri-
> umphs over your mere idea of her. And you want her to;
> you want her with all her resistances, all her faults, all her
> unexpectedness. That is, in her foursquare and indepen-
> dent reality. And this, not any image or memory, is what
> we are to love still, after she is dead.

> But "this" is not now imaginable. In that respect H. and
> all the dead are like God. In that respect loving her has
> become, in its measure, like loving Him. In both cases
> I must stretch out the arms and hands of love—its eyes
> cannot here be used—to the reality, through—across—all
> the changeful phantasmagoria of my thoughts, passions,

and imaginings. I mustn't sit down content with the phantasmagoria itself and worship that for Him, or love that for her.

Lewis seems right about this. But he names a challenge that I don't know how to meet.

One way I have tried to meet it is to gather, greedily, perceptions and stories of Linda from others who knew her, who saw sides of her I rarely saw. I grieve that I will never again be startled by her unpredictable, utterly singular self, surprising me again, giving birth to new dimensions of our love, revealing new facets of the diamond.

Day I: Close of the Day [Compline]

[Sung]

In manus tuas, Domine,	Into your hands, O Lord
Commendo Spiritum meum:	I commend my spirit:
Redemisti me, Domine,	For thou hast redeemed me, O Lord,
Deus veritatis.	God of Truth.

—ROMAN BREVIARY

Day I: Night [Vigil]

Out of the depths I cry to you, O Lord.
Lord, hear my voice!
My soul waits for the Lord
more than those who watch for the morning,
more than those who watch for the morning.

—PSALM 130:1–2A, 6 (NRSV)

Time is the canvas
Stretched by my pain.

—RILKE

Grief's Anguish: Night throws darkness over the grieving soul. Daylight sometimes makes it possible to see through the fog of sadness, but nighttime drives out that one grace. Nighttime is the hour of grief's anguish. Nighttime can happen any hour of the day. Sometimes, as Rilke puts it, grief encases me like a massive rock:

> I am so deep inside it
> I can't see the path or any distance:
> everything is close
> and everything closing in on me
> has turned to stone.

It is like nothing else in my experience; I am unable to get my bearings, movement seems impossible.

> Since I still don't know enough about pain,
> this terrible darkness makes me small.

In my grieving, I have allowed sadness in the door when it knocked. But grief's anguish never stands politely at the door. It doesn't knock, it doesn't announce itself. It bursts in, bludgeons me, grabs me by my jaw and reaches down into my stomach and pulls my gut inside out. Grief's anguish is raw, utterly physical. It rudely shoves thought entirely out of the room. It is mindless and mad. Uncontrollable. Demonic. I am in its power, powerless; suspended, lifted off the ground and out of time. I am unable to see beyond the moment, unable to see. The cries echoing from the walls around me startle me with their ugliness.

The pain continues to wave over me!

Stop it, O God,
please stop it!
. . .
I think I'm in control,
but I can't stop
the undulating ache
that wells up suddenly
and overwhelms me
until I collapse
from grief.

—ANN WEEMS

Grief's anguish can be conjured by a thought or memory, by the to-do list found in the bedside table, the unfinished knitting on the closet shelf.

Remembered happiness is agony;
so is remembered agony.
I live in a present compelled
By anniversaries and objects:
your pincushion; your white slipper;
. . .
the label *basil* in a familiar hand;
a stain on flowery sheets.

—DONALD HALL

It takes nothing more than touching something of hers to blow the door wide open. One of the most powerful attacks of grief's anguish came when I brushed against one of Linda's favorite jackets hanging in the closet next to my sport coat.

Grief, at its deepest, is physical. Utterly, frighteningly physical.

"How much does matter matter?" the poet Mary Jo Bang asks. "Very." is her simple answer.

What I want desperately is Linda's touch. The pain of its absence is sharper than the thrust of any knife.

The pain is evident in the icon of the Lamenting Virgin.

Lamenting Virgin (Theotokos Threnousa)

The depth of the virgin's grief is evident in her deep-set eyes; too deep, it seems, for tears. Yet it is not her countenance that expresses the deepest truth of grief; it is her gesture. The inclination of Mary's head and the position of her hands recall other, much more familiar icons. In one, *Theotokos Eelousa* (Virgin of Compassion) or *Theotokos Glykophilousa* (Virgin of Tenderness)—like the Lady of Vladimir—Mary holds the infant Christ tenderly in her arms and inclines her head to receive a kiss from the infant, who reaches his hand to her neck. Another, a form of the pieta, the *epitaphios threnos* (lamentation upon the grave), depicts Mary cradling the head of the dead Christ who has just been removed from the cross. In the first, the joy and love of mother and son are palpable. Yet, in some versions, the virgin's eyes are sad with the knowledge of the passion to come. In the second, Mary again holds the body of her beloved, now sacrificed and lifeless, but still in her arms. In the *Lamenting Virigin*, we encounter gesture again, the love and sad tenderness is there, but, in the place of the beloved Son there is emptiness. "Alone she saw to birth as now she has seen to the burial. She took and held the precious child and prepared the undefiled body for the grave." But the arms are not just empty; the arms are perceptibly in motion, drawing the absent One closer to her breast.

I know no more powerful, no more achingly truthful depiction of the persisting experience of grief than this. All the gestures of love I had learned over the years are hollow after Linda's death. Meant to surround her, to make my heart known to her, my arms now ache from the emptiness. The weight of such emptiness has no measure.

And yet, there is more to the message of this image. For it is the infant so tenderly held that gives the gesture its meaning. The virgin's inclination, bearing, and being are shaped by the love in that gesture. Her love, even in her time of absence, is formed around her beloved, a love returned with equal tenderness and depth by the infant Christ. Likewise, although the absence of the infant, and of the dying Lord, can never be denied, the very shape of the virgin's love makes the beloved almost visible.

Lady of Vladimir

Epitaphios Threnos

Day II

Day II: Dawn [*Lauds*]

God speaks to each of us as he makes us,
then walks with us silently out of the night.

—RILKE

Diary Entry: August 5, 2008—7:45 a.m.—Seattle

IT IS A NEW morning. I thank God for mornings. Night brings
dark thoughts and weariness of soul. The new day brings with it
a prospect of joy in life, perhaps for new possibilities, for a new
way to walk these days with my darling. I truly hope so, because
walking without her is deepest pain.

Linda and I kept this familiar prayer at our bedside:

This is another day, O Lord.
I know not what it will bring forth,
    But make me ready, Lord, for whatever it may be.
If I am to stand up, help me to stand bravely.
If I am to sit still, help me to sit quietly.
If I am to lie low, help me to do it patiently.
And if I am to do nothing, let me do it gallantly.
Make these words more than words . . .

—BOOK OF COMMON PRAYER

Day II: Daytime

Ungiven gifts pile about me.
Unsung songs remain
trapped in my throat.
Unsaid words lie rotting
in my mouth,
and I sit staring down
a lifetime of unlived days,
for love didn't leave
when death arrived.

God, what will I do
with the unfinished love?
It wells up within me
with nowhere to go,
and I am bursting
with the pain of it.

—Ann Weems

Unfinished love. Love is never finished, of course, but our love was still deepening, still maturing. As her illness progressed, I sensed a greater tenderness in Linda's touch and glance. The memory of them now is precious; painful but sweet. During her illness I learned difficult lessons about caring, about how to help her cope with her struggles. I have not finished the course, but the unfinished work of love now has a different assignment. The work is harder, because Linda can no longer gently correct my course. I won't let this stop me, though.

I have done some things to keep alive what she most cared about. I have been working with a national organization to promote lung cancer research to which she dedicated her life. I am also seeking ways to honor her courage and compassion, her insight into the needs and suffering of others, her steadfast refusal to tolerate behavior that denies respect for the vulnerable, her always evident grace and patience.

While she now rests from her caring labors, her deeds follow after her (Rev. 14:13). Our love, unfinished but firm, will continue to live and grow.

Day II: Mid-Morning [Terce]

Diary entry: August 3, 2008—9:30 a.m.—On Amtrak train
in mid-North Dakota

YESTERDAY'S TRAVEL WENT SMOOTHLY. After leaving my bags at Union Station, I walked around downtown Chicago, our hometown. It was a beautiful, sunny, cool day. Chicago was splendid, but Linda's absence was painfully present to me. I hope that someday the memories of our precious times together here will be welcome and lovely, but now they just bring pain—pain at her loss, pain at my loss of her and of the joy of sharing these good times.

The train left Chicago promptly at 2:15 p.m. My compartment is small but private and comfortable. I share meals in the dining car with other passengers. We engage in pleasant conversation while looking out on the passing countryside. Thus far, the trip has been all I could have hoped for. It is very comfortable, very relaxing . . . but bipolar. One moment I delight in the beauty of the passing scene, in the sense of relief and relaxation, in Trollope's *Orley Farm*; the next moment I am weeping, stunned by a sense of loss and a desperate wish to have Linda at my side. She is gone! I hold her close to my heart, but she is gone. How can that be? It must not be! I refuse to accept it!

Day II: Noon [Sext]

What is left but this:
The compulsion to tell.

—MARY JO BANG

HOW CAN I KEEP Linda near me? So far, I have found only one way that works. I talk about her—to anyone, everyone; in private, in public, to anyone who will listen. When I do, she is present to me. Talking about her can so fill me with joy that the pain can't break through. I talk over the pain; I shout it down. Doing so, I risk her scolding. I hear her telling me to get control of myself, to stop boring people. But I know that I do not bore them. How could they be bored? I would not allow it. She doesn't believe me. Even so, I would rather endure her scolding than live silently in her overwhelming absence. When I am alone, lost in the dwelling-place of her absence, unable to separate, if only for a few moments, the joys of our life together from the pain of her absence, that is when I totter on the edge of grief's anguish.

Day II: Afternoon [None]

What do they celebrate in the sanctuary, O God?
And of what do they sing in joyful procession?

...

How can I join their singing, O God...?

—ANN WEEMS

WHY CELEBRATE, INDEED? IN many churches it is customary to put away the Alleluias during Lent. I remember singing "alleluia" at the conclusion of Linda's funeral. It affirmed her and her life as much as it sent praise to the One who promised to hold her when I could hold her no longer. But I find it increasingly difficult to celebrate now. And it's hard for me to understand how others around me can.

Diary entry: August 4, 2008—9 p.m.—Seattle

I ate dinner at an Ethiopian restaurant tonight. It was a memorable meal, but like so many other experiences during this trip, the pleasure of the meal was hung with the heavy, rough cloth of Linda's absence. Grief obliterates the pleasure and when it fills all the space in my heart, I can't help wondering why I am doing this. I have planned this trip and lots of other things over the last two months, not for the pleasure I hope to take in them, but just to keep myself moving on. I am surprised to discover that often I am inclined to withdraw quite fully from life. This trip and my work push me on, despite my reluctance, but I don't want to go on living without my darling. It is so very empty and joyless.

Day II: Twilight [Vespers]

C. S. LEWIS WRITES that grief feels like suspense because of "the frustration of so many impulses that had become habitual."

> Thought after thought, feeling after feeling, action after action, had H. for their object. Now their target is gone. . . . So many roads lead thought to H. I set out on one of them. But now there's an impassible frontier post across it. So many roads once; now so many *culs de sac*.

Not suspense, I think, but angry disappointment, apprehensiveness, and fear. I have repeatedly taken these roads. Sometimes by choice, but many other times against my choice, I find myself on the road, and suddenly the road falls away to nothing, not a *cul de sac*, but a great abyss. I feel a vivid, terrifying sense of vertigo, of falling—not my falling, but *Linda's*.

Day II: Close of the Day [Compline]

O Christ, you wept when grief was raw,
and felt for those who mourned a friend;
come close to where we would not be
and hold us, numbed by this life's end.

The well-loved voice is silent now
and we have much we meant to say;
collect our lost and wandering words
and keep them till the endless day.

—JOHN BELL

Day II: Night [Vigil]

How could I not have saved you . . .
How can I not reach where you are
And pull you back. How can I be
And you not.

—MARY JO BANG

WHEN I AM ALONE, almost every thought of Linda, no matter initially how lovely and joyful, brings me back immediately to that last, terrible, unstoppable day. I had so little time with her that day. I spent most of it arguing with the insurance company over their refusal to cover hospice care, eventually signing papers and making arrangements with the hospice people, ordering a hospital bed, oxygen, drugs, moving furniture to accommodate the hospital bed, driving to the pharmacy to pick up the drugs. I had no time to pause, no time to sit quietly, no time even to sense that taking a moment to sit quietly was what was most needed. Linda was struggling, in great pain. She was in her last few hours. I didn't see it. When she needed me most, I was not there.

I relive that day a thousand times over, the same madness, the same overwhelming sense of desperation. She is falling into some awful darkness. I stretch out the whole length of my body; the stretching is acutely painful. She is falling . . . out of my reach.

The most difficult struggle for me these early months has been to break the stranglehold of *that day*, of that falling. It crowds out every other thought of her except one: I want her back.

God, give her back!

Day II: Night [Vigil] II

THE PROBLEM IS NOT that we are not together now. We have lived apart for lengths of time. I know what it is for her to be distant. It's rather the terrible and terrifying finality of her being gone. Like water spilled on the ground, life lost cannot be gathered up again.

I weep for what was
and will never be again.
I weep for a future
that is no longer possible.
I weep because I love.

—ANN WEEMS

It's the terrible neverness of death, as Wolterstorff says. Never again to share a meal, never again to talk quietly about what worries or pleases us, never again to share a moment of pride in our newlywed children, to hope for the future, to celebrate the past.

Never again.

Never.

Day III

Day III: Dawn [Lauds]

Tell me you caught him
in your arms
and wiped the tears
from his eyes,
and showed him your face
as you had showed him
your heart.
Tell me you are always
with us
in life and in death.

—ANN WEEMS

[Sung]

Die mit Tränen säen, werden mit
Freuden ernten.

Sie gehen hin und weinen und
tragen edlen Samen,

und kommen mit Freuden und
bringen ihre Garben

—BRAHMS,
EIN DEUTCHES REQUIEM

Those who sow with tears shall
reap in joy.

They go out weeping, bearing
precious seeds

and return with joy bearing
their sheaves.

—FROM PSALM 126:5-6

Day III: Mid-Morning [Terce]

I saw *Wheatfield with a Reaper* in the Van Gogh Museum during a visit to Amsterdam in September, 2007, nine months after we first learned of Linda's lung cancer. I found the painting to be especially powerful and, in its paradoxes, encouraging.

Vincent van Gogh, *Wheatfield with a Reaper*

On the flight home to Linda a few days later, I wrote these thoughts about the painting:

"Van Gogh saw the reaper as death working feverishly to complete its task under a blazing sun. It is noteworthy, however, that the reaper is not represented in the conventional "grim reaper" manner, a hooded, skeletal, morbid creature, but rather as an ordinary, hard-working peasant, almost friendly in mien. Similarly, the target of his reaping, "humanity" in van Gogh's vision, is not old and decrepit, but rather vibrant, vigorous, youthful in its ripe maturity. At first this struck me as especially sad, as if death is cutting down those who are most fully alive—all too soon. But, van Gogh's vision in this painting, or at least the vision it suggested to me is not mournful, but encouraging and life-affirming. The field of vibrant humanity is vast, vital, bursting with life, dwarfing the reaper and, I think, resisting the reaper's efforts. I cannot help thinking that that vibrancy—with the help of the (divine?) burning sun which sustains its life and makes the work of the reaper even harder—will prevent the reaper from completing his determined task. There is no guarantee; the reaper has partially succeeded and some of the wheat has fallen to his scythe. But there is also hope."

I have kept a copy of this painting with me ever since. It hangs in my study. It sustained me, especially as Linda's health visibly declined in the last three or four months of her life. It sustains me now, albeit with a very different hope.

Day III: Noon [Sext]

The experience of grief is universal. We inherit a vocabulary semantically and culturally appropriate for the occasion. Some of it is profoundly helpful, some of it profoundly inadequate, and some of it simply falls somewhat short of the mark. In the latter category is the word "widower." I have as much difficulty thinking of myself as a widower as my forty-year-old cousin once had thinking of herself as a grandmother. "Grieving spouse"— yes, but that's just a part of the story. "Former caregiver"—another part of the story, but it underplays my participation in the struggle. "Survivor" has taken on positive significance in the cancer "survivor community." Many of my friends in the North Carolina Lung Cancer Partnership wear it, justly, as a badge of courage. Sometimes, I introduce myself as "a kind of survivor" or "co-survivor," because I continue daily in my struggle with the monster that afflicted us both and transformed our lives. But I don't feel like merely a survivor. I feel more like a committed combatant, as Linda did. When she died, she did not "lose her battle with cancer," she completed her part in the struggle; and she commissioned me to continue the fight. So, what I am is . . . a "champion"—*Linda's champion.*

[Fund-raising email message I sent to friends around the world.]

Fall, 2008
Dear Friends,

Throughout her long battle with lung cancer, Linda saw herself as a kind of pioneer. She found meaning and courage in the thought that her struggle would help in some small way to advance understanding of this dread disease and discovery of ways to treat it effectively. One way that I have sought to carry on her mission is through participation in the work of the North

Carolina Lung Cancer Partnership, which seeks to raise aware-ness of lung cancer and raise money for research in this area.

I am involved in planning the Partnership's "Free to Breathe" 5k run/walk scheduled for November 8 in Raleigh. I invite you help me raise money for lung cancer research through support-ing this event. It is very easy for you to pitch in. Just visit my fund-raising page at . . .

Please join me in honoring Linda and the passion that gave the last years of her life focus and direction.

Gratefully,
Jerry

Day III: Afternoon [None]

*Diary entry: August 4, 2008. Monday—8 a.m.—Western
Washington Mountains*

It's a beautiful morning. I rose early to shower and get to breakfast. Yesterday was a very good day. I had pleasant conversations with other passengers over meals, a "wine and cheese experience" in the afternoon, and three long stops in small towns of North Dakota and Montana. Over dinner, I met a man whose wife died of cancer twelve years ago. He seemed to be enjoying life. Maybe that is possible for me in the future. Since about 5 p.m. yesterday, the scenery has been very beautiful. We skirted Glacier National Park, and now we are making our way through the Cascade Mountains of Western Washington. I look forward to seeing Seattle and Vancouver, but I will miss the pace and style of traveling by rail.

I am sure Linda would have loved this trip. It would have been too physically demanding for her in the last few months, of course, but before then it would have been possible. She always wanted to travel west—especially to the Grand Canyon—even more so after she became ill. I was reluctant. We never seriously considered train travel. I regret that now. We would have had a wonderful time together. I so wish I could share this experience with her now. We were cheated—she was cheated—of some of the best times in life. Lately, I am weighed down with regrets, especially regrets about how little time I allowed for us to do things together. I loved her deeply, and I truly took pleasure in those times. Why was I so blind and absorbed in things that now seem insignificant?

Day III: Twilight [Vespers]

Misery is sociable, it loves company. But grief's suffering is solitary, isolating.

People reach out to me: "Yes, I lost my brother earlier this year . . ." I smile, but inside I shout, "It's not the same! Can't you see?" It cannot be. *Linda* died. This utterly unique, infinitely precious life has ended. There is *nothing* comparable.

> So many are alive who don't seem to care.
> Casual, easy, they move in the world
> as though untouched.
>
> —RILKE

O vos omnes qui transitis per viam:	Is it nothing to you, all you who pass by?
adtendite et videte si est dolor sicut dolor meus.	Look and see if there is any sorrow like my sorrow.

> —LAMENTATIONS 1:12 (NRSV)

What strikes me as utterly incredible, beyond my grasp, is not just that this sorrow is unlike any other sorrow, but that people out there, all those who pass by, cannot sense the gaping hole in the universe. Aiwara no Narihira, the ninth century Japanese Tanka poet asked, "Can it be that there is no moon or that spring is not the spring of old, while I alone remain the same person?" I ask the reverse question: Can it be that there is yet another moon, that autumn is the same autumn of old, when all of life it is radically and forever changed? "In the vacancy," Mary Jo Bang wrote, "the world went on revolving." Impossible.

It seems that the problem, the root of my isolation, lies not just or even primarily in others. It lies in me. I have lost the center of my life and, sometimes, it is impossible for me to resist the feeling that nobody cares—even when, at the same time, I repeat to myself that many around me have, time and again, gone out of their way to demonstrate their love and caring. This feeling is impossible to resist because Linda's absence fills all the space in my mind. For the moment, I cannot imagine the caring of another person. I cannot imagine it, until it is physically present to me. Job's friends got it just right at the beginning: They sat on the ground with Job seven days and nights without saying a word to him. "For they saw that his suffering was very great" (Job 2:13). They just sat on the mourning ground, alongside their friend; they didn't try to do something, or fix what was broken, or, for heaven's sake, to explain it. (Isn't it always ultimately for heaven's sake that the explanations are given?) They just sat with Job.

Often when I observe people going about their daily lives, it is easy for me to imagine them connected to others with thin, steel-strong, elastic threads woven into a thick net of relations of caring and concern. I could almost see the threads in the sunlight. Sometimes, I feel as if someone has taken a scissors to the fabric and cut all the strands that hold me in place. At other times I feel that, when Linda, the center of my network, was removed, the fabric was rent top to bottom. When this feeling comes over me, I can't think my way back into that network. But when those who love me actually sit on the mourning ground with me and listen to my sighs and sobs, I can almost see new threads stitching me back into the fabric.

The dwelling place of absence is profoundly physical; only physical presence, I think, can help to fill the void.

Day III: Close of the Day [Compline]

As the day closes around me, I can't escape the shadow of regret.
No, not mere regret—guilt: the terrible sense of having failed the
one I love.

What will the coming darkness hold in store?

> Keep me as the apple of your eye;
> hide me in the shadow of your wings.
> Lighten my darkness, Lord.
> Let the light of your presence
> dispel the shadows of night.

> —THE BOISIL COMPLINE

Day III: Night [Vigil]

Silver-toothed traps, their springs tightly wound and rust free, lie in my path wherever I turn. In the grip of one, I cannot escape the thought that I have failed her, especially in her last days. What was on her mind that Saturday and Sunday before she died? Had she resolved already to let go? Was she preparing herself? Why did I not recognize it? How could I have helped her? Did she know I was there to hold her hand and give her courage for her choice?

Did she know that I had not abandoned her?

Did she know that I would have gladly traded places with her?

When Linda was ill, I tried so very hard to walk the balance beam between smothering care and worried acceptance of her need for independence. I failed, often. Of course, I tried as hard as I could. But that's no comfort now. It wasn't then. To know that I failed the one I love without measure, however small the failure might have been in the eyes of others, adds another leaden weight to the already unbearable sack of regrets I carry.

And when the trap has sunk its teeth deep into my soul, I'm held fast, forced to face forward, as a stern clerk rises to read out particulars of a life of failures, hurts, wrongs, betrayals. The list is endless. No detail is left out. No time is left for rebuttal, for qualification, for mitigation.

What is far worse, I didn't even have time to ask her forgiveness. Forgiveness. Forgiveness is what I need most now. Friends remind me that Linda generously and completely forgave shattering wrongs done to her by others; that it was deep in her nature to look beyond those wrongs to the love they stained and distorted. Surely, they say, she has long forgiven you who were more precious to her than her life, like the father in the parable, who ran out to meet his beloved son. Yes. I believe that. But I still need to hear it . . . from her. Without that, how can I forgive myself?

My longing for her forgiveness runs deep. It hurts . . . almost as much as her absence.

Rembrandt van Rijn, *The Homecoming of the Lost Son*

[Sung]

Erbarme dich,	Have mercy Lord,
Mein Gott, um meiner Zähren willen!	My God, because of this my weeping!
Schaue hier,	Look thou here,
Herz und Auge weint vor dir	Heart and eyes now weep before thee
Bitterlich.	Bitterly.

—J. S. BACH, ST. MATTHEW PASSION

Day IV

Day IV: Dawn [Lauds]

For you created my inmost being;
    you knit me together in my mother's womb. . . .
My frame was not hidden from you
    when I was made in the secret place,
    when I was woven together in the depths of the earth.
Your eyes saw my unformed body;
    all the days ordained for me were written in your book
    before one of them came to be.

      —PSALM 139:13–16 (NIV)

But now thus says the Lord, he who created you,
O Jacob, he who formed you,
O Israel: "Do not fear, for I have redeemed you:
I have called you by name, you are mine.
When you pass through the waters,
I will be with you;
and through the rivers, they shall not overwhelm you;
when you walk through fire you shall not be burned,
and the flame shall not consume you.
For I am the Lord your God, the Holy One of Israel,
Your Savior."

      —ISAIAH 43: 1–3A (NRSV)

Since we began our struggle with cancer, and especially after Linda's death, baptism has come to mean a great deal to me. It was one major theme I insisted that we include in Linda's memorial service. We used Psalm 139 and Isaiah 43. That naming and claiming, that promise—"Linda, child of the covenant"—binds us tightly together. It is a promise that even now I hold God to keep. "You promised!" I say every Sunday morning as I enter the sanctuary and pause at the baptismal font, and later as I stand in the memorial garden where Linda's ashes lie.

There is another reason baptism has become so important to me. I have come to see it as a symbol of the wonderful grace of the relationship Linda and I had since we were teenagers. We were set off on a journey together way back then: choosing each other, but also, and more deeply, chosen for each other. Only now, almost forty-five years later, I am beginning to realize the depth and wonder of this fact.

Day IV: Mid-Morning [Terce]

For those who are joined to all the living there is hope. So writes the Preacher (Ecclesiastes 9:4). This phrase expresses, with precision, the truth of Linda's experience and mine during her long illness. It continues to be true for us. Our hope lies in her being joined, inseparably to all the living, and the Living One, who loves her.

I was asked to say a few words in worship one Sunday morning about what it is to be "joined to all the living" in community. I started with these familiar words from the book of Lamentations:

> The steadfast love of the Lord never ceases, his mercies never come to an end; they are new every morning; great is your faithfulness. "The Lord is my portion," says my soul, "therefore I will hope in him."

> —LAMENTATIONS 3:22–24

I continued:

For many years, these words moved and comforted me. And during Linda's illness and since her death, they have had special meaning and depth for me. But I have also long found them deeply puzzling. For they occur in the very center of the book of Lamentations. In the midst of the most profound, life-shattering, utterly devastating dark valley of loss, how is such a profession of hope possible?

Over the two and one half years of Linda's illness, I have been given a clue to the puzzle. In the valley of the shadow of death, the writer of Lamentations, the utterer of profound laments, must have been surrounded and sustained by a community of God's people.

In baptism, God names us and claims us, God makes us—each one of us—children of the covenant, a covenant that promises steadfast love; a covenant renewed every morning. But also, at every baptism we—this community—acknowledge that we are parties to this covenant; we—each one of us—pledge to each other to be bearers of God's steadfast love.

If you want to see the face of God's steadfast love, turn to your left . . . to your right . . . look behind you. Through Linda's long illness, so many of you wrapped her and me in your love and concern and prayers. You gave us courage and hope and the sure knowledge that even in that dark and frightening period God was with us.

And when, finally, Linda and I entered the valley of the shadow of death, God's never ceasing steadfast love encircled us: in our living room, around her bed, you gathered.

This, my dear friends, is one very important reason why we gather, why we are gathered here. Our worship together and, yes, our stewardship, sustains us and sustains this community as ministers of God's steadfast love.

Day IV: Twilight [Vespers]

Hugo Simberg, *The Wounded Angel*

Two boys bear an injured girl through Helsinki's Eläintarha Park toward the Blind Girls' school and Home for Cripples in what seems to be a funeral procession. The younger boy in front has resigned himself to that role; the older boy in the back resists, determined but fearful.

I came across this intriguing, enigmatic painting, by the Finnish symbolist painter, Hugo Simberg, while Linda was visiting her parents, just three months before she died. Her mission on that visit was to convince her father that the time had come to put her mother, also suffering from cancer, in hospice care. Linda was, for me, the angel of mercy, suffering wounds we can see and deeper wounds we cannot see. Like Linda, the wounded angel is unable to see very far ahead: her vision is obscured by the rough bandage around her head and the boy in funereal black. Her energy is nearly spent, having put it all into bringing comfort to those whose love she knew, understood, and freely returned. She did not demand perfection of that love. She reconciled the ill-matched threads of that love and wove them gratefully into a single cloth. Now she was in need of carrying, and care.

When I first found this painting, I especially loved it because it gave me a role to play. Standing behind her, bearing her weight gravely but proudly, I was ready to punch anyone who threatened to do her harm. I saw myself as her protector, her champion. But now, when gripped by the trap of guilt, I began to see in this angel of mercy also an angel of forgiveness.

From this I have learned two things—or rather I have seen dimly two things, and I'm still learning their significance. First, forgiveness does not wash away the wrong; it does not make the relationship white as snow. It does something far more remarkable, and beautiful. Forgiveness weaves the wrongs together with other strands of the relationship so that they no longer dominate and distort it; but rather, reconciling the ill-matched threads, some of them ugly in their own right, and integrating them into the whole, forgiveness redeems them and in redeeming them strengthens the fabric. It may not be as pretty as we might have hoped, but in its imperfection it is stronger and more resilient. I have also learned that forgiveness is lived, not just given (although it is surely a gift), lived by the forgiver and also by the forgiven. When I most long for a word of forgiveness from Linda, I look at how she lived and how she loved me, how we lived and loved together. For now, that will have to do.

> I shall accept my regrets as part of my life, to be numbered among my self-inflicted wounds [Wolterstorff writes]. But I will not endlessly gaze at them. I shall allow the memories to prod me into doing better with those still living. And I shall allow them to sharpen the vision and intensify the hope for that Great Day coming when we can all throw ourselves into each other's arms and say, "I'm sorry."

> The God of love will surely grant us such a day. Love needs that.

Day IV: Close of the Day [Compline]

But Zion said, "The Lord has forsaken me,
    my Lord has forgotten me."

Can a woman forget her nursing child,
    or show no compassion for the child of her womb?
Even these may forget,
    yet I will not forget you.
See, I have inscribed you on the palms of my hands. . . .

—ISAIAH 49:14–16A (NRSV)

I know in my heart that
you will not forget me.
Your grace is all-encompassing,
and your love has no conditions.
You, O God, will not forget me,
for you have made covenant with me,
and your covenant is forever and ever.

—ANN WEEMS

Day IV: Night [Vigil]

Grief isolates the one grieving from others, but it much more effectively isolates one from the beloved. Wolterstorff thinks that sometimes, through tears, we might be able to "see things that dry-eyed [we] could not see." Through tears, perhaps, but not when one is in the iron grip of grief's anguish. Grief's anguish pushes everything out. Lewis knew this. "[P]assionate grief," he writes, "does not link us with the dead but cuts us off from them." This has been my experience. It is still almost impossible for me to bring any memory of Linda to mind, when grief is my only focus: the wrenching pain blurs the memory, *and her*, beyond recognition. She comes into better, if not altogether clear, focus when I try to speak with others about her. Lewis writes that when the overwhelming intensity of his grief subsided a bit, he was able to remember his beloved "as if the lifting of the sorrow removed a barrier." "It is just at those moments when I feel least sorrow . . . that H. rushes upon my mind in her full reality, her otherness."

Good for him. That's not where I am. It must take a whole lot more strength, or more time, or something else, to get to that point. Only pain floods in now when she appears. After all, Linda is dead, and our life together—our daily, physical interaction, sharing of thoughts and hopes, fears and joys—has ended, abruptly and without recovery. There is no joy in that.

Day V

Day V: Dawn [Lauds]

In December, seven months after Linda died, I discovered Pablo Neruda's love sonnets, through the work of soprano, Lorraine Hunt-Leiberson, who recorded five of the sonnets in settings by her husband, Peter Leiberson. I was first drawn to her work because of the intense emotion and deep beauty of her singing in recorded performances of Bach's setting of the *Nunc Dimitis*, "*Ich Habe Genug*" (BWV 82), which I happened to buy a few months after Linda died. Her singing on this recording is exquisite and powerful. I sensed a depth of understanding that was not just a matter of superb musicianship. I tried to find out more about her, and I learned that a number of her CDs were recorded while she was fighting cancer. She recorded Leiberson's setting of the Neruda sonnets on November, 26, 2005, seven months before she died.

I admired her, not just her singing. But I felt more than admiration, I think. I was repeatedly drawn to her recordings just to catch a faint glimpse of Linda's spirit. Listening, I recalled Linda on the good days, when she climbed the seemingly endless stairs to our seats in the basketball stadium to watch her beloved Tar Heels play, when she was enthralled with the beauty of the Carolina ballet, when life held good and beautiful things for her and for us, and the suffering could be put out of mind for a while. I bought Hunt-Leiberson's recording of her husband's five Neruda sonnets. One, the last of the set of five, especially caught my attention:

[Sung]

> My love, if I die and you don't—,
> My love, if you die and I don't—,
> Let's not give grief an even greater field.
> No expanse is greater than where we live.

I was so moved that I sought out the whole set of Neruda's *Cien sonetos de amor*. I took the collection home from the library one evening. I looked through the first dozen or two. Lovely, I thought.

I put the collection aside, on my bedside table.

Day V: Mid-Morning [Terce]

When she was very young, our daughter Alicia had a bedtime ritual that she played out mainly with Linda. It went something like this:

Alicia: "Goodnight, Mommy, I love you."

Linda: "I love you more."

Alicia: "No, you can't, cuz I love you as far as counting goes up to."

Linda: "Well, I love you even more than that!"

Alicia (triumphantly): "No you don't, cuz counting never stops!"

Day V: Noon [Sext]

I recall a Sunday during her illness. Linda was in the middle of chemotherapy, but holding her own. She came into the sanctuary in an elegant hat and matching outfit. Standing with the choir in the narthex, I watched her enter and take her seat next to K., her "pew pal." To a friend standing nearby I said, "Have you ever seen such a beautiful woman in your life!"

Day V: Afternoon [None]

In the fall before Linda died, I was doing some work in Amsterdam. I acutely felt the separation from Linda. Sitting in Vondelpark in the early evening, I watched people strolling by—families with young children, noisy teenagers, pierced and tattooed drifters down on their luck, a couple of young lovers for whom the world around them did not exist. I was struck how little each of them seemed to appreciate the utter fragility of life, how little they seemed to pay attention to the darkness just around the corner, and how little they seemed to be aware of the unutterable preciousness of life. Then I began to realize that their blindness itself was a precious gift. Life lived every day in painful awareness of its fragility can be a burden, a distraction from the joy and meaningful business of life.

Yet, the psalmist prays, "Teach us to number our days that we may gain a heart of wisdom" (Psalm 90:12 NIV). Where's the wisdom in numbering our days, I wonder? Perhaps it lies in the thought that if we treat our days as innumerable, as inexhaustible, they lose their meaning and value for us. Unnumbered days are fungible; to lose a day, by entirely ignoring it, is no loss because any number of days remains to compensate the loss. "Not to worry, there are lots more where they came from," we are inclined to think. In this path, surely, lies no wisdom. Rather, days numbered, that is, days counted, count. Focusing on the end may be debilitating, but ignoring the significance of each day is equally so.

So then, should we live just one day at a time, as those facing grave illness often feel forced to say in public? This, despite its appearance of homespun wisdom, is not entirely sound advice, at least not in my experience, or Linda's, I think. It is not the way to live vitally, vigorously, with dignity and courage in the face of mortal challenges. It is to surrender, to allow illness to steal one's future. To live humanly and with meaning is to live with tomorrow as well as today in mind, to give the days of our lives an arc, a direction and focus, to make its momentary minor and major tones into a melody. In a melody each note must be valued; to lose or silence any constituent note is to lose the melody. So, finding a way to compose a melody out of the notes available to us is a way of meaningfully numbering our days. Therein, perhaps, lies hope of wisdom.

Day V: Twilight [Vespers]

I have found it difficult to accept talk of "healing after your loss." This way of talking goes wrong in two ways. First, it gets the focus of grief all wrong. It focuses on me, on *my* loss, *my* pain. This entirely misses the point of the pain. The point, the inescapable point is: Linda is dead! This fact cannot be changed, corrected, or compensated for over time. It's an awful, utterly unacceptable fact. If my suffering is someday diminished, that awful fact remains unchanged; so why would I want my suffering to diminish? It stands witness to the fact that she is dead and that *that's* the problem. If there is loss to be accounted, surely it is hers. Linda is dead—the word hits the bottom of my heart like molten lead. To this, only one response is conceivable, only one reaction is physically possible: No! Every day, one hundred times a day, I say *No! No! No!*

Who will chant the mantra when I am no longer able? I pray that God does. After all, God promised! God promised steadfast love to hold Linda, to surround her and to affirm her intractable, independent, infinitely precious reality.

The second problem with talk of "healing" is that it looks at grief as dysfunction, pathology. Surely it is not! Grief is love's protest. "We don't really want grief, in its first agonies, to be prolonged," Lewis writes, "nobody could."

> But we want something else of which grief is a frequent symptom. . . . What we want is to live our marriage well and faithfully. . . . If it hurts (and it certainly will) we accept the pains as a necessary part of this phase. We don't want to escape them at the price of desertion or divorce. . . . We were one flesh. Now that it has been cut in two, we don't want to pretend that it is whole and complete. We will be still married, still in love. Therefore we shall still ache. But we are not at all—if we understand ourselves—seeking the aches for their own sake. The less of them the better, so long as the marriage is preserved. And the more joy there can be in the marriage between dead and living, the better.

The hard, painful labor of grief is just part of the labor of love, of keeping love vital and growing. I am left to perform this labor on my own. So be it. Linda did far more than her share for thirty-nine years. She loved as far as counting goes up to. I have some catching up to do.

Day V: Close of the Day [Compline]

Keep watch, dear Lord,
with those who work or watch
or weep this night,
and give your angels charge
over those who sleep.

Tend your sick ones, Lord Christ;
rest your weary ones,
bless your dying ones,
soothe your suffering ones,
pity your afflicted ones,
shield your joyous ones,
and all for your love's sake.

—BOOK OF COMMON PRAYER (SLIGHTLY REVISED)

Day V: Night [Vigil]

Undo it, O God! Give her back!

> O God, why did you create a life
> that includes death?
> Why did you create us
> to love one another
> and then take from us
> the ones we love?
>
> —ANN WEEMS

Give her back! If I can't have her back, I don't care to go on.
The pain is too raw, too deep, too unrelenting. I see no end.

> I'm slipping, I'm slipping away
> like sand
>
> slipping through fingers. All
> my cells
>
> are open, and all
> so thirsty. I ache and swell
>
> in a hundred places, but mostly
> in the middle of my heart.
>
> I want to die. Leave me alone.
> I feel I am almost there—
>
> where the great terror
> can dismember me.
>
> —RILKE

Grief's Liturgy

I have been saying *no* for so long: *no* to the monstrous cancer that ravaged Linda's body; *no* to the radical transformation of our lives and shriveling of our future; *no* to her death that cut short a life and love that was infinitely precious. I have been saying *no* so long that it has become hard to keep this *no* in focus, to keep it from becoming an equally powerful *no* to my own life. Why has my anguish at Linda's death so often been accompanied by the terrifying sense of her falling? Am I afraid of falling, into an even deeper anguish? Words of the "Dies Irae" echo in my head: *Domine . . . libera [me] . . . de profundo lacu, . . . ne cadant in obscurum*—Lord, free me from the deepest pit, let me not fall into this terrible darkness.

Day VI

Day VI: Dawn [Lauds]

Diary entry: January, a few days after Linda's birthday

Grief's anguish gripped me again last weekend. For two days, I was in the darkest, most profound lake of agony and despair I have known since Linda died. I could not pull myself out. Late Sunday night, unable to sleep, I idly picked up the book of Neruda's love sonnets that was lying on my bedside table. I paged through them, but the tears blurred the words on the page. I wanted nothing of life. It hurt to weep. It hurt to breathe. Through dark, bitter tears, I read:

"When I die . . . I want you to live . . ."

It was Linda's voice! Soft, but unmistakable.

I read the words again. I heard her voice even more distinctly. My eyes cleared enough for me to read the rest of the poem:

When I die, I want your hands on my eyes:
I want the light and wheat of your beloved hands
to pass their freshness over me once more:
I want to feel the softness that changed my destiny.

I want you to live while I wait for you, asleep.
I want your ears still to hear the wind, I want you
to sniff the sea's aroma that we loved together,
to continue to walk on the sand we walk on.

> I want what I love to continue to live,
> and you whom I love and sang above everything else
> to continue to flourish, full-flowered:
>
> so that you can reach everything my love directs you to,
> so that my shadow can travel along in your hair,
> so that everything can learn the reason for my song.
>
> —PABLO NERUDA

I wept again, but with relief.

I *can* live, I thought. I can live *with her. Together* with her. I can be her eyes, her ears. I can live by loving what she loved, what we loved. I can sing her song, full-voiced. I can sing an "alleluia."

My eyes were drawn to another sonnet just a few pages on. Reading, I heard Linda say:

> If I die, survive me with such a pure force
> you make the pallor and the coldness rage;
> flash your indelible eyes from south to south,
> from sun to sun, till your mouth sings like a guitar.
>
> I don't want your laugh or your footsteps to waver;
> I don't want my legacy of happiness to die;
> . . .
> Absence is such a transparent house
> that even being dead I will see you there,
> and if you suffer, Love, I'll die a second time.
>
> —PABLO NERUDA

Through these new and very different tears, I was able to see what, dry-eyed, had been only darkness to me.

That night Linda returned to me. God's wounded angel said to me, "Let's go. . . . Give me your hand. Let's live again, together."

Day VI: Mid-Morning [Terce]

Lately, I have sensed a change in my attitude toward this struggle of living and finding some meaning in Linda's absence. The struggle through the worst of times during her illness was difficult, but we had each other. I drew strength from her strength and from the clear conviction that she and I were involved together in an all-out struggle with a powerful, terrible, but nameable common enemy. A monstrous, unequivocal evil stood opposed to us. We faced it and fought it together. Since Linda's death, I have felt alone, left to battle demons on my own. But even more, I have found it difficult to name the enemy. The enemy is not the pain, since pain seemed to be the truest witness to the place Linda had in my life. The enemy is not *my* loss or loneliness, although God alone knows how vast that loneliness is. What I protest is her *absence*, or rather *her* absence. The enemy is not *death*, but *her* death. What I reject is *her* death. It is unutterably wrong. Not a wrong to me—a wrong *to her*, perhaps; to the impoverished world, perhaps—but not specifically *to me*. So, who is, or what is, the enemy? With whom or with what am I to do battle? I am moved by the example of Linda's courage, but what does courage call upon me now to do? These questions had no answers for me and I could not go on without answers.

I still don't understand the profile of this enemy, but I sense a gradual change happening to me. I have come to feel less abandoned, less left alone to fight through the pain and desperation. I have a gathering conviction of Linda's partnership in this struggle. When I weep, as I often do, I do not weep quite alone. Also, I have come to see, still dimly, that I may not need to find and name the enemy to battle, the monster to slay. I have come to think that maybe the courage I am called on to muster is just the courage to hold fast to the conviction that what she most loved is still worthy of our energy and effort. I could not have begun to understand this without her help. "Love what I have loved," she whispered. She taught me that perseverance in the face of a bleak future, finding joy in it, is not a denial of what she means to me, but my most ardent affirmation of her and of our love.

So my struggle now is to recover those things she loved, the things we loved, the things that enabled us to flourish even when the times were hard. It is easy to lose my grip of this twofold conviction. Most nights are not graced with the sound of her voice. Many nights bring more pain than promise, and her love seems a distant country. But I have heard her speak. She touched my battered and wounded heart and gently turned my eyes away from the wounds, to the things we loved and celebrated—none of them more important than the love we have for each other.

Day VI: Midday [Sext]

Take him, earth, for cherishing,
To thy tender breast receive him.
Body of a man I bring thee,
Noble even in its ruin.

—Prudentius

Donatello, *Magdalene Penitent*

Diary entry: February 13—Florence, Italy

After lunch, I left work to spend an afternoon with my darling. Nine months ago today she died. I have been anxious about the arrival of this day. Other such monthly reminders have laid me low. But today was, on the whole, a lovely day. I treasure these times we spend together. I tried to find something beautiful to fill our afternoon; not a difficult task in Florence. I decided to visit the Academy—home of Michelangelo's *David*—but when I arrived, I learned it was closed due to a wildcat strike called by museum staff. Disappointed, I walked down the street to the Museo dell'Opera del Duomo, which displays much of the cathedral's art. Two unforgettable pieces captivated me: Michelangelo's unfinished *Pietà* and Donatello's very late, haunting wood carving of Mary Magdalene. The *Pietà* is powerful, raw, and muscular. It lacks the refinement of the version in St. Peter's Basilica, but makes up for it in sheer power.

However, it was Donatello's *Magdalene Penitent* that made the deepest impression on me. It struck me to the core. Mary is emaciated. The sharp bones of her cheeks and chest are visible, her long hair is matted, her clothes hang limp. She is at the end of a life of the deepest and most savage, body-assaulting and soul-wrenching trials. Yet her hands, and especially her eyes, reveal a depth of faith and profound serenity; her struggles set them deep, but they reveal a source that sustained her. The eyes ennoble her. She looks directly into the face of death, neither with terror nor with resignation. She seems to know something or understand something not accessible to me.

Today Linda led me to a new realization of the extraordinary beauty of her life, and especially the beauty and grace of the way she lived out her last days. If it hadn't been for the random strike by the museum staff at the Academy I might well have missed Donatello's *Magdalene*. Some months ago I thought that I would never again be startled by Linda. Wrong again.

Day VI: Afternoon [None]

Dirary entry: February 6, 2009—Florence, Italy

I decided that I needed time, unencumbered by the demands of work, to spend with Linda. So, at the beginning of the year, I took a year's personal leave from my work. I decided to visit places we loved. I arrived in Florence a few days ago for an extended stay. I'll be working some here, of course, but my time will be my own . . . ours. I am determined to do things not just *for her*, in her honor, but *together with her*. To be her eyes and ears and to rediscover the things we enjoyed together. Florence has a special place in our history. We visited it thirty-five years ago. We were very young. I was a graduate student and Linda was caring for Alicia, who had arrived just a few months earlier. We didn't have more than a dime to our names, but we had love, and a child, and hopes.

Tonight, after dinner at a small restaurant, I strolled without destination in the old city, as we loved to do. The city seemed unfamiliar to me until I found myself in Piazza Signoria, in front of Palazzo Vecchio. Memories of our visit years ago returned, laced with sadness. We were so young then; life was full of promise and peril. We had no sense that our time together would be short, far too short for a life as beautiful as hers. She and I grew over those years, and we grew together. My love, deepened over these years, will not let her go. I know she won't let me go, either.

Diary entry: February 14, 2009—Florence, Italy

Another joyful day spent being Linda's eyes. I wandered the city for most of the day. I visited Santo Spirito Church, then Santa Maria del Carmine, and its Brancacci Chapel with wonderful frescoes by Masaccio and Masolino. Then I walked along the Arno, and finally climbed the hill to Piazzale Michelangelo, a broad, open piazza overlooking the city of Florence. It was a very steep climb, but the view was spectacular. Looking to the north and east we could see Tuscan mountains beyond the city. Just above the piazzole stands San Miniato church, one of the great gems of Florence, a serene and sacred place of green and white marble. Above the high alter is Christ Pantocrator in splendid mosaic. I returned by way of the Basilica di Santa Croce church. The piazza outside the church is ringed by shops and a restaurant. It may have been from one of the gold merchants in Piazza di Santa Croce where, thirty-five years ago, we bought twenty-four carat gold earrings for Linda. It was a reckless splurge. We could not afford them on a graduate student's stipend. A few years later Linda was devastated when she discovered she had lost one of them. But, turning loss into treasure, she had the remaining earring made into a wedding band, which she wore almost every day over the next twenty-five years. She had a knack for making awkward and awful things right and precious.

Diary entry: Late March, 2009—Lucca, Italy

This is my last weekend in Italy before I return home. I visited the medieval-renaissance town of Lucca, which is not far from Florence. Around the old city is a wide, earthen wall. On Saturday, an early spring garden fair was being held on the wall. All sorts of plants, trees, and garden equipment were set out for sale, stretching for more than a kilometer. Amidst all this work of the earth and for the earth, there stood one booth with handcrafted items for sale. A woman from Venice was selling hand painted silk. I stopped, captivated. The work was exquisitely beautiful and lovingly executed. After standing a long time admiring the work, I walked on. But after wandering the town I found myself drawn back to the walls around the city and to the booth. I spent a very long time just taking in what I knew delighted Linda. "I want what I love to continue to live / and you whom I love and sang above everything else to continue to flourish, full-flowered" (Neruda). My heart was moved knowing she was seeing it through me.

One piece, a silk table scarf with large, hand-painted purple irises, was especially beautiful. I decided to buy it for Linda. "Is this a gift?" the lady asked. "Well, . . .yes," I said. She wrapped it carefully in special paper and tied it with a wide purple ribbon. I took it home, still wrapped, packing my suitcase carefully around it. I gave it to Alicia. "Mom wanted you to have this," I said, "until she sees you again."

Day VI: Twilight [Vespers]

Vincent van Gogh, *At Eternity's Gate*

... the wall between us
Is very thin. Why couldn't a cry
from one of us
break it down?

—RILKE

> Between the living world
> and the world of death
> is a clear, cold pane;
> a man who looks too close
> must fog it with his breath,
> or hold his breath too long
>
> —WENDELL BERRY

I have long loved van Gogh's sketch, *At Eternity's Gate*. The artist worked at least three versions of it; in addition to the one above, he did a lithograph in half-figure and, in the last year of his life, painted a version of it. I had it nearby during Linda's illness, but, unlike van Gogh's *Wheatfield with a Reaper*, this image struck me as not fitting for our experience at that time. It represented to me the time, probably in hospice care, when we would face death together. We never had that time. I recall talking about this image with my brother shortly after Linda's funeral. I said that it no longer speaks to me, because that time—waiting at eternity's gate—is past. However, over the last several months I have come to understand the image in an entirely different way.

In his *Four Quartets*, Eliot seeks to capture in a series of images the illuminating, life-shattering, life-shaping experience of what he calls "intersection time," when the transcendent breaks through the mundane—"the intersection of the timeless with time." He explores:

The luminous, haunted rose garden of "our first world";
The dance at the "still point of the turning world";
Time when "the kingfisher's wing . . .
        [answers] light to light";
"Communication of the dead . . . tongued with fire
        beyond the language of the living";
"Midwinter spring," "suspended in time"—
        "springtime but not in time's covenant";

Love, itself unmoving, causing movement, timeless
     "caught in the aspect of limitation";
and Incarnation.

Woven in with these images are equally telling images of darkness:

The dark night of the soul;
Darkness of God, darkness without God;
Darkness of abandoned, empty, silence; but also
Darkness pregnant with presence.

The moments in this intersection time are sudden, unexpected, fleeting, and often recognized, dimly, after they pass. But once they have passed and been recognized, time and experience before and after are transformed. Eliot sought through poetic image and paradox to alert us to the lurking possibility of intersection time.

Van Gogh's sketch of the old man sought to do the same, I think. The old man, in deep sorrow, overcome, and ennobled, is at "eternity's gate." Eliot thought that "to apprehend / the point of intersection of the timeless / with time, is an occupation for the saint." Maybe he meant "for the blessed." After all, Christ said, "Blessed are they that mourn." *If* there is any blessing in mourning, and there is powerful evidence against such a thought, it lies not in the comfort, or not in the comfort alone. Rather, the blessing and the comfort lie in the recognition that comes to one who sits alongside the old man, recognition that the suffering, loss, and even the death itself may be redeemed. Without denying the death or minimizing the suffering, without losing sight of the appalling awfulness of the suffering and the death, it is possible in some moments to recognize through tears that the brutal denial of all that is precious is answered, and that which is of value beyond price is affirmed. According to Psalm 130, "out of the depths" comes personal recognition that "with the Lord there is steadfast love," love that has "great power to redeem."

However, this very recognition contradicts all that we know. We are creatures of here and now, of blood and bone. All that we know, and—if we are honest with each other and ourselves—all that we can conceive, is embodied and temporal. Matter matters. It is touch that touches the heart, and touch is, for all we know, in and of time—time that is allotted to us in small and shrinking packets. Is it a surprise, then, that encounters at intersection time, while they promise to affirm and redeem, can equally bring one to the edge of darkness? For they put one face to face with the end of all that we can know and conceive. "Human kind cannot bear too much reality," says the bird as it rushes the poet out of the rose garden in Eliot's *Burnt Norton*; the "enchainment of past and future woven in the weakness of the changing body protects us from reality we cannot endure." Are the darkest agonies of grief's anguish the shudders of a time-enchained changing body unable to bear reality? Perhaps the anguish comes from holding one's breath too long on life's side of the cold pane.

Yet, if the price of safety, of avoiding the greedy reach of demonic agony, is foregoing any further opportunity of hearing Linda's voice through the wall, feeling the light breath of her touch, and both of us hearing again the covenant promise that her suffering is redeemed, I will not pay.

Day VII

Day VII: Dawn [Lauds]

Diary entry: Holy Saturday, 2009

Today is the most difficult of the days of Holy Week, the day of God's death, descent into the abyss. In the past I have worked to understand something of the sense of abandonment that the Marys felt, which drove them to the tomb Sunday morning. No need this year. Now I reside in the dwelling place of absence. Today, instead, I tried to fill that void by doing things we needed to do, mundane chores I had saved up for months. As I went from shop to shop, I could feel Linda cheering me. "Good job. We really needed to get that done." I felt triumphant! The significance of the utterly mundane was affirmed.

Today, as so often over the last few months, I have felt Linda's caring, her watching over me, her affirmation—the pain is still there, but something pulls the sting and gently lays a cool cloth on the wound.

Day VII: Daytime

Andrei Rublev, *Holy Trinity*

Rublev's transcendently beautiful vision represents the perfect circle of the Trinity in the eucharistic feast, eternal communion in love and sacrifice. The table forms a chalice with Christ, regally attired, in its center, accepting the commission of the Father, while the Spirit of steadfast love, promises serene comfort. The Oak of Mamre, symbol of life, sinks its roots in the chalice. The dance of these Three Persons is the dance at the still center of the turning world that Eliot had in mind. It is a communion feast prepared for the entire world, the feast in which those held in God's everlasting arms now participate.

Diary entry: Easter Sunday, 2009

I knew there would be an early Easter service in the church's memorial garden this morning, so I planned to arrive well ahead of time to prepare myself. This was to be the first service I attended in the garden since we interred Linda's ashes there last July. In the service of committal we celebrated communion. Today, at this early Easter service, both *communion* and *baptism* were celebrated. The pastor asked me to participate in the baptism, representing the Session. This was a deeply meaningful experience in view of what baptism has come to mean to me, especially over this past year. In that place, where Linda's ashes lie, and her name is inscribed on the wall amongst the saints of the congregation, we enacted God's baptismal covenant to little "K." and recalled the promises made so long ago to Linda and me to hold us in love forever. We celebrated communion, the seal of that promise.

After the service in the memorial garden was finished, I stayed behind to spend just a few minutes alone with Linda. I took the leftover bread and spread it over the place where her ashes lay and took the wine and poured it out there. Today, Linda and I again dipped bread in the same cup. The steadfast love of the Lord embraced us both. Drawn in to that perfect circle, we participated in the feast together.

Every Sunday, and especially Easter, Christians celebrate the resurrection. The theology of resurrection, Christ's unique resurrection and the creed's hoped-for resurrection of the body, offers difficult thoughts. We Christians struggle with them. However, the message of the resurrection is crystal clear and powerful. The resurrection, like the incarnation, reminds not only of God's emphatic *No* to death and suffering, but also God's equally emphatic *Yes* to creation and to the lives of God's covenant partners—a *Yes* that resounds through that creation and is reflected in the lives of each of us. God "has made everything beautiful in its time" (Eccl 3:11), which, as Barth reminds us, allows each of us to share in the meaning and content of all created time, even those times that are not our own.

Day VII: Twilight [Vespers]

Can anything be said about the "terrible mystery of death"? I don't mean the self-imposed alienation from God that so much concerns New Testament writers, but rather the ineluctable, absolutely final end of the life of a cherished human person. The anguish of loss felt by those of us who remain is difficult to communicate and awful to experience, but it is not as much of a challenge to the mind and heart as the fact of death itself is. The fact of death is a challenge with such sharp edges and such self-dwarfing proportions that, for most of our lives, we use every means available to push it aside. But it is harder to do that when one is forced to stare death in the face.

For those who have thrust all mystery out of range of their attempts to understand life and the world, for those who live in a thoroughly disenchanted world, there is no mystery in death. They may understand why we are inclined to hate death, but they see in it no fundamental threat to life. But those of us who are unable to see the world, at least that part of the world that we have loved utterly and by which we have been loved likewise in return, as devoid of the enchantment of unconditional value, and especially, those of us who are unable to understand the world and our place in it except as the creation of an infinitely loving God—*we* find death to be a deeply troubling mystery.

The problem for us is twofold. Death seems to stand as a root and branch challenge to the goodness of God's creation, especially God's creation of living and loving human persons and the goodness of those persons affirmed by the incarnation. "O God, why did you create a life/that includes death?" Ann Weems asks. Likewise, it appears to challenge our understanding of the absolutely, unconditionally precious nature of those whom we love. For death demonstrates decisively the limited, conditioned quality of this nature and so, it would seem, of its value.

Karl Barth offers a serious response to this twofold challenge. He does not deny that death is the end of the person who, as he put it, once was not, who then lived and loved, and then is no more. He does not place his hope in the eternal living of the human person, for, in his view, to be human is to be temporal and to be temporal is to be subject to a natural end as well as a natural beginning. But, he argues, this is neither a denial of ultimate value of the human life thus lived or of the person who lived it, nor of the goodness of the creation or the Creator. It is, on the contrary, the very condition of that life and its value. For it is only as temporal that human beings are able to be partners—covenant-partners—of God; creatures capable of participating actively in a relationship with God. It is this relationship, in his view, that is the ground of the unconditional value of each person.

Moreover, he continues, the truth and persistence of this value does not depend on the unending existing of the life bearing that value; for it is affirmed, acknowledged, and honored, unconditionally and eternally, by the eternal God. God holds each of us in love, before the foundations of the world and after our lives have moved into the past. In so doing, God ensures neither an eternal being for us—for that mode of being is fit only for God—nor an unending life, but rather a complete, fulfilled life. Resurrection is a matter of life's completion, not its endless continuation. Not a life that is eternal, but a life that is eternally affirmed, honored, and loved; and, thus, completed, through being affirmed, honored, and loved by the incomparably good God. In this way, one who has been, but is no longer, shares in the eternal life of God.

Barth's thoughts capture part of what I have long believed is the core of the doctrine of baptism and its significance for our understanding of death. Yet, this response to death's challenge, for all its merits, does not fully answer the challenge that death poses to our understanding of the value of life and of the lives of loved ones we cherish. It explains the persistence of valued human lives despite their temporal termination. But this persistence is entirely and literally *sub specie aeternitatis*. That is, human life is completed and held eternally to be completed in the eyes of

God; however, the cherished person, whose life is thus completed and honored, does not seem to participate in this appreciation. It is a completion that leaves out the person whose life is thereby completed, because to be such a person is to be in a position to grasp and appreciate at least to some extent this very value.

So, Barth's proposal leaves us with a choice. Either we fall back on the orthodox idea that we exchange this life for an eternal life, or at least everlasting living—an idea that is simply beyond our understanding because our understanding is necessarily limited to life and living rooted in our time. Or we accept that our joy and comfort lies in the here and now—recognizing, understanding, and appreciating that, in the words of St. Paul, nothing, not even death, can separate us from the eternal love of God, that God's light illumines the lives we have lived even when they are past, that God's love treasures them, and that God's own sacrifice and suffering redeems our suffering and loss. In either case, it would seem to be true that God's faithfulness holds us in life and in death and beyond death.

Have I made any headway penetrating the mystery of death? Not a lot, perhaps. But, then, explanation of the mystery is not what I most want. Of course, what I most want is Linda, here and now, to love and to cherish. But if that is not possible, then I call on God to do what I can no longer do adequately, what I could not do adequately even when Linda was at my side and in my arms. Dear God, in your infinite love, hold her in your everlasting arms!

Day VII: Close of the Day [Compline]

Where can I go from your Spirit?
      Where can I flee from your presence?
If I go up to the heavens, you are there;
      if I make my bed in the depths, you are there.
If I rise on the wings of the dawn,
      if I settle on the far side of the sea,
even there your hand will guide me,
      your right hand will hold me fast.
If I say, "Surely the darkness will hide me
      and the light become night around me,"
even the darkness will not be dark to you;
      the night will shine like the day,
for darkness is as light to you.

          —PSALM 139: 7–12 (NIV)

one whose darkness
is darker than night,
    . . . keeps vigil with no candle.

          —RILKE

Day VII: Night [Vigil]

The night is a huge house
where doors torn open by terrified hands
lead into endless corridors, and there's no way out.

—RILKE

O dark, dark, dark, amid the blaze of noon,
Irrecoverably dark, total Eclipse
Without all hope of day

The Sun to me is dark
And silent as the Moon
When she deserts the night
Hid in her vacant interlunar cave.

—JOHN MILTON

Diary entry: May 3, 2009

It has arrived, the month of Linda's death. As Mary Jo Bang wrote, I "teeter / On the brink of a date marking more / Sorrow in store." Sure enough, as if on schedule, grief's anguish struck again. I was putting away the basket of cards and notes I received after Linda's death, and I stopped to read a few of them, and then a few more. I thrilled through quiet tears to read again these celebrations of her grace, kindness, and gentle presence. The tears were sweet. But then the image of Linda's last day, that terrible unstoppable day, brutally shoved everything good and lovely out of my mind. It took control, again. Terrifying, black, empty, suffocating, falling.

C. S. Lewis writes that losing the beloved is like losing one's leg. In time, perhaps, the pain subsides and one learns to get around on crutches, but the leg is permanently gone: "I shall never be a biped again." A few pages later Lewis writes: "Tonight all the hells of young grief have opened again; the mad words, the bitter resentment, the fluttering in the stomach, the nightmare unreality, the wallowed-in-tears . . .[H]ow often will the vast emptiness astonish me like a complete novelty and make me say, 'I never realized my loss until this moment'? The same leg is cut off time after time. The first plunge of the knife into the flesh is felt again and again."

I don't suppose I will ever stop feeling this anguish, or fearing its return. The risen Christ kept his wounds, Wolterstorff reminds us. Perhaps my wounds will also remain. They are part of who I am now. But I also know that I am not just these wounds, that I carry Linda in the strong, and rich, and vital part of my soul too. When I see, she delights; when I sing the melody, she sings a descant. Partners. For life.

Day VII: Close of the Day II [Compline]

O Lord, my heart is not lifted up,
my eyes are not raised too high;
I cannot lift them,
　　　the weight of my tears is too great.
I do not occupy myself with things too great for me
Because my mind is filled with terror and foreboding,
　　　with images of that unstoppable day.
Calm and quiet my soul, dear God,
like a weaned child with its mother.

Day VIII

Day VIII: Daytime

Diary entry: May 13, 2009

One year ago today Linda died. When Linda was ill, we measured our joy and relief in weeks. Now a year has passed. I have been anxious about the arrival of this day. I was determined not to let grief's anguish take control. It was impossible not to feel the full weight of this day, but I worked to fill the day with activities that affirmed our life together. This morning, I contacted the development officer at the cancer center to learn how the endowment I established last summer in Linda's name was being used. I also spent time planning a party for the end of the month to celebrate our fortieth wedding anniversary. I put together a guest list, began thinking about food, and looked through pictures I might gather into a slide show for the party.

I also slowly went through the house, holding each piece of pottery we had collected over the years, letting it speak again of the places we visited and the life we shared—Makkum, Deruta, Williamstown, Sea Grove, Cedar Creek Pottery in Creedmore. I held them close. Their physicality moved me deeply—aching, but comforting. I have found that memories even when wholly joyful are incomplete. I need to *touch, to embrace*. If I am denied the opportunity to caress and embrace her, I will caress and embrace what is hers. The round firmness of the vase, the rough texture of the numda, and the sweet softness of her afghan responded. It was inadequate, yes, but still comforting, offering some nourishment for my hungry heart.

I spent the afternoon—three hours of it—gathering fragments of our life together before cancer struck her. I drove through Hillsborough, to north Orange County, through our former neighborhood, past the house we loved, then down to the clubhouse opposite. I sat in the parking lot and looked across the field at our house and let the memories flood in. Tumbling over each other in quiet confusion, they were poignant, beautiful, painful, joyful memories lost to me until that moment, stolen by Linda's cancer. Greedy and resentful, I snatched some of them back.

After thirty minutes I drove on to explore again the country roads we cycled and walked for years. The infamous and demanding Terry Road, beautiful Kiger Road, Mary Hall Road—where a man once stopped, seeing Linda walking on the side of the road, and asked, "Ma'am, just out walking for your health?"—Little River Road, and the Little River Presbyterian Church, Law's Store Road, Hawkins Road, Walnut Grove Church Road with the lovely stone church. . . . The countryside was resplendent, extraordinarily beautiful. Linda and I moved out near the country ten years ago, in good part to enjoy this pastoral landscape. We took such pleasure biking and walking these roads, and in each other's pleasure in it! The drive was sheer delight. Each curve, crossroad, pasture, and vista conjured sweet memories. Today, I recalled much of our seven years before cancer. For a little while, I was Linda's eyes, gathering in for her and with her many fresh and vivid reminders of a beautiful time in our life together.

Day VIII: Twilight [Vespers]

And all shall be well, and all manner of thing shall be well.

—JULIAN OF NORWICH

Those who have fallen into the hell of grief's anguish and have been pulled out again, those who wear the wounds and feel their pain again and again as if for the first time, can, perhaps, dare to say those words. My brother reminded me once that Lewis Smedes saw the work of grace in this. Smedes wrote:

> I walked away from Cal's hospital bed, opened the door, and stopped for a moment to look back before I left him. He lifted his head a bit, smiled, and said, "It's all right." And then I left him and never saw him again. But his words have haunted me ever since and have become for me a metaphor of life's deepest question. How can anyone really believe that it is all right when everything is hopelessly wrong? . . . How can we be ground down in pain and grief and death and still believe that it's all right at the center of life? The answer must be blowing somewhere in the winds of grace.
>
> Grace does not cure all our cancers, transform all our kids into winners, or send us all soaring into the high skies of sex and success. Grace is rather an amazing power to look earthy reality full in the face, see its sad and tragic edges, feel its cruel cuts, join in the primeval chorus against its outrageous unfairness, and yet feel in your deepest being that it is good and right for you to be alive on God's good earth. Grace is power, I say, to see life very clearly, admit it is sometimes all wrong, and still know that somehow, in the center of your life, "It's all right." This is one reason we call it amazing grace.

Day VIII: Close of the Day [Compline]

Come to me, O Comforter,
come to me.
Hold me against the pain
for just awhile
so that I might catch my breath.

—ANN WEEMS

Day VIII: Night [Vigil]

Diary entry: May 13, 2009

It happened again. That monster, grief's anguish, took hold again tonight. Despite some sad moments in our old neighborhood earlier today, the day I spent with my darling was good and beautiful. But tonight, something very dark and frightening took over on my way home from choir rehearsal. As I was leaving the choir room, I began to feel very strange—disconnected from the people around me, on a different emotional plane, in a different universe. I felt angry, resentful. Don't they realize what day it is? In the car on the way out of the parking lot, I broke down. I wept. I wailed. I screamed *"No! No! No!"* all the way home. As I was driving, I looked at the dashboard clock: 8:30 p.m.—the last few minutes of Linda's life.

Arriving home, I lost all control. The pain was as deep and raw and overwhelming as it has ever been. I felt again, as I did a few weeks after Linda died, that her death was happening all over again, and again she was slipping out of my grasp. Falling . . . Desperately, I reached out to grab her, to hold on to her. Again, she slipped away. I paced the house, but suddenly I was unable to walk into the dining room. The sight of the bedroom just beyond where she died repulsed me so powerfully that it was impossible to go farther. A stiff arm in my chest would not let me pass. All my breath and will were sucked out of me. I was terrified. I retreated to the kitchen, sobbing, wailing. After some time, I don't know how long, the burden lifted, almost as suddenly as it fell on me. I stood, trembling. I took a step. With effort, I walked into the dining room, then into the bedroom. The monster retreated.

I was left exhausted, utterly at a loss. Not long after, Alicia called. I felt calmed by her words and the tone of her voice, and was able to sleep through the night. I woke in the morning feeling as if I had battled food poisoning overnight. This is the terrifying part of the hard work of grieving. When these times hit, I feel so utterly out of control, completely overtaken. I know pain is the reverse side of love, and I do not wish to deny the pain, but never again do I want to experience the agony of last night. I have no idea why some think that in suffering we have a vision of God. This suffering is black, monstrous, demonic. God help me if it strikes again. I don't know whether I can survive it.

Day IX

Day IX: Dawn [Lauds]

[Sung]

Ihr habt nun Traurigkeit; aber ich will euch wiedersehen und euer Herz soll sich freuen und eure freude soll niemand von euch nehmen (John 16:22).

Ich will euch trösten wie einen seine Mutter tröstet (Isaiah 66:13).

—BRAHMS, *EIN DEUTCHES REQUIEM*

These words, especially "*Ich will euch trösten wie einen seine Mutter tröstet,*" (I will comfort you as a mother comforts her child) accompanied me daily during Linda's illness. I sang Brahms' requiem with the Choral Society in the spring of 2007. I would repeat these words as I walked in the dark mornings before work and at night before I fell asleep. At my request, our choir sang this moving section of the requiem at Linda's memorial service. I repeated these words again and again as I struggled for sleep the night of the first anniversary of Linda's death.

Day IX: Mid-Morning [Terce]

It ceased to hurt me, though so slow
I could not feel the Anguish go—
But only knew by looking back—
That something—had benumbed the Track—

—EMILY DICKINSON

Diary entry: May 15, 2009

Reflecting on the events of the anniversary of Linda's death, I am encouraged by the fact that it was possible for me, most of the day, to focus on what was and is most precious in our lives together. The dark and demonic had hold of me only for a short time, maybe no more than an hour, not several days, as it did a few months ago. Also, never in that darkest of times was I inclined to give up on life itself. In fact, I felt as if I were fighting for my life. This is surely Linda's doing, her strength, her gift. She also has enabled me to see that those times of anguish, when I was gripped by a terror I cannot name and felt an overwhelming wish for life to end, were not the reverse side of my love for her, but something demonic, not prompted by love. She let me see that our love is vital, engaged with life, drawing from it all the goodness it has to offer, facing its evil as a part of that life as well. Our love for each other was always and ever a love of life, a life together, of course, but a love of life.

Day IX: Daytime

He Qi, *Peace Be Still*

On that day, when evening had come, he said to them, "Let us go across to the other side." And leaving the crowd behind, they took him with them in the boat, just as he was. . . . A great windstorm arose, and the waves beat into the boat, so that the boat was already being swamped. But he was in the stern, asleep on the cushion; and they woke him up and said to him, "Teacher, do you not care that we are perishing?" He woke up and rebuked the wind, and said to the sea, "Peace! Be still!" Then the wind ceased, and there was a dead calm. He said to them, "Why are you afraid? Have you still no faith?" And they were filled with great awe and said to one another, "Who then is this, that even the wind and the sea obey him?"

—MARK 4: 35–41

Christ, who tamed the waters of chaos at creation, stills the chaotic and demonic. In our terror, he seems to be asleep, hidden, uncaring. Our terror blinds us to his presence, our fear and pain obscures the memory of his steadfast love. Unlike the voice in Job's whirlwind, this Creator is present, incarnate; subject to the wind's buffeting like us, present with us in our vulnerability. Even more, he who calms the chaos is also he who stretches out his arms in suffering love. The dove reminds us of the covenant as it lays a crown of thorns on the head of the crucified Christ.

Day IX: Twilight [Vespers]

Instead of explaining our suffering God shares it.

—WOLTERSTORFF

There are at least two "problems of evil." One is *theological* or *philosophical*: the *argument* that the existence of evil makes in the court of the mind against the idea and hence the existence of a good and gracious God. This problem can shake the faith of the thoughtful individual, and sometimes drive faith away; it is also a convenient brief for those who have no faith, to excuse when an excuse is needed to give faith no further attention. The other problem of evil, the *existential* problem, is in a way more fundamental. It does not challenge an idea or prove a point. It doesn't challenge or threaten to change a set of beliefs. It threatens to change a relationship, with God, with oneself, and with others. This is the problem of evil that Job faced. And to me, the answer he was finally given was, on the surface at least, an answer to the wrong question. To the anguished question, "Why did you do this? Why did you do this to me; but even more why *to them*, the vulnerable and oppressed, the one's you promised to protect?" the whirlwind answers, "because I can, and it fits into an order of the universe you can never understand."This answer misses the point of the question. For the problem was not puzzlement about goodness or power, but about commitment and compassion, and about covenant. God's apparent injustice and cruelty does not lead Job to deny God's existence. Job's orientation to God is too fundamental for that. But it threatens completely to change his relationship with God. Job's wife's advice—"Curse God and die!"—precisely addresses this existential problem. The point of cursing God is not defiance, but withdrawing from an intolerable relationship, a relationship that, from everything Job could see—and his friends added nothing to what he could see for himself—was broken beyond repair.

Death and the evil of death, it seems to me, is not a challenge to faith—if, by that, one means *belief* in God's existence, or the coherence of the idea of God. I'm a philosopher. I had puzzled about this long before Linda died. And it will continue to puzzle me until I cannot be puzzled any more. But that question is a world of experience away from the challenge Linda's death posed. When she died, I didn't want an explanation—I still don't. An explanation, especially if it is a compelling one, would be intolerable. There is no explanation, no argument, no demonstration—not in a philosophical text, a holy book, or a whirlwind—that could fill the hole in my soul and in the world left by her death. I don't want an argument—I don't want to debate or wrestle with God or anyone else—I just want Linda back. I stagger—and, if it only knew, the world too staggers—from her loss. If her return is not possible, I want someone to sit at my side and try to understand why I find that to be intolerable, utterly and forever unacceptable. I need someone to feel that raw pain, to hear the uncontrollable shrieks it forces out of me, to join me when I say a hundred times over *No . . . No . . . No.*

I don't want to know *why*. I want to know *who*. *Who* is there to feel with me this utterly unique pain at the loss of this infinitely precious person? *"O vos omnes!"* If God cannot, or chooses not to, do that, then all bets are off; the relationship is already shattered, there is nothing I can do to fix it. I won't deny God's existence. What would be the point of that? But I can't continue to live in that relationship. It's too dangerous, too costly. He can't be trusted. I'm not even sure life is worth living any more.

One thing Job's story leaves out, however, is that the God who made and measured and calmed the chaos in the beginning, also suffered, and still suffers. God knows the appalling awfulness of death from the inside. Not just in the way that I know it—although he wept with Martha and Mary at their brother's tomb—but in the way Linda knows it. So, when God says, "Yes, I know, I lost a loved one, too," the words don't ring hollow like when the guy down the street said them. When God says the words, they are not just a blundering attempt at empathy. Rather, God's words are a quiet reminder of his infinite capacity for collecting Linda's suffering, and my suffering, in a cup that he inscribed with our names on it.

> God, You named us and claimed us. You held us in your arms before we could speak or walk or listen or love.
>
> You made Yourself vulnerable to our pain and to our waywardness.
>
> Gather all the suffering Linda endured, keeping it to herself when she lived,
>
> but which after her death settled like a heavy dust on everything.
>
> Accept all the raw and wrenching anguish I still nurse in my gut.
>
> I know You won't deny it or minimize it, or, for God's sake, explain it.
>
> I know You acknowledge it for the life and the love and the infinite goodness it bespeaks.
>
> You made Linda, Your icon, and You made her beautiful.
>
> Take her suffering and by embracing her with Your infinite caring, redeem it.

Day IX: Close of the Day [Compline]

Calm me, O Lord, as You stilled the storm.
Still me, O Lord, keep me from harm.
Let all the tumult within me cease.
Enfold me, Lord, in Your peace.

—THE FELGILD COMPLINE

Day IX: Night [Vigil] . . . yet again

Diary entry: May 30, 2009

For most of this month, I have been planning an anniversary celebration, celebrating not the anniversary of Linda's death, but rather our fortieth wedding anniversary. Tonight was the night. The house was full of friends, many of whom had known us for nearly thirty years. Among the guests were some who had not been back to our house since they held vigil with us the night Linda died. The celebration was joyous. Holding hands, Linda and I made our way from one group of friends to another, sharing stories, hugs, laughter, and tears.

Then, slowly, in twos and threes, the guests left until all were gone and the house was empty. Again, I was back in the dwelling place of absence. I wept.

Will it always be that the sweetest presence is followed, overfilled, by absence?

I wept again. But not as one without hope.

> And all shall be well and
> All manner of thing shall be well
> When the tongues of flame are in-folded
> Into the crowned knot of fire
> And the fire and the rose are one.

—T. S. Eliot

[Sung]

Agnus Dei, qui tolis peccata mundi,	Lamb of God, who takes away the sin of the world
Dona nobis pacem	Grant us peace

—Bach, *B-Minor Mass*

References

Introit I

"Sleep, O sleep"—"The Ebba Compline," in *Celtic Daily Prayer: A Northumbrian Office* (New York: HarperCollins, 2005), p. 41.

Introit II

"We are summoned"—John Bell, "Since We Are Summoned," in *The Last Journey: Songs for the Time of Grieving* (The Iona Community: Wild Goose Resource Group, 1996).

"Set[ting] it all in order"—From "Requiem for a Friend," in *The Selected Poetry of Rainer Maria Rilke*, edited and translated by Stephen Mitchell (New York: Random House, 1982), p. 73.

"the terrible mystery of death"—From the funeral hymn used in the Greek Orthodox funeral service written by John of Damascus. (John wrote: *"Terror truly past compare is by the mystery of death inspired."*)

"such shattering of love"—Nicholas Wolterstorff, *Lament for a Son* (Grand Rapids, MI: Eerdmans, 1987), p.43.

"intersection time"—T. S. Eliot, "Little Gidding," in *Four Quartets* (New York: Harcourt, Brace, Jovanovich, 1971), line 105. The garden reference is to "Burnt Norton" in *Four Quartets*, lines 20–43.

Introit III

"*Selig sind, die da Leid tragen*" Matthew 5.4 (Luther Bible, Deutchen Bibelgesellshaft, 1984). Brahms opens *Ein Deutches Requiem* with these words.

Day I: Dawn

"I have always known"—"Narihira LVI" in Kenneth Rexroth, trans., *One Hundred Poems from the Japanese* (Verona, IT: New Directions, 1955), p. 58.

The phrase "My dearworthy darling," sometimes attributed to the fourteenth century poet Richard Rolle's meditation on the passion, "My truest treasure so traitorly was taken." See *Richard Rolle: The English Writings*, Rosamund S. Allen, trans. (New York: Paulist Press, 1988), p. 206, n. 19.

Day I: Noon

"Loud as a trumpet"—Rainer Maria Rilke, *Rilke's Book of Hours*, translated by Anita Barrows and Joanna Macy, (New York: Riverhead, 2005), p. 205.

"I would have painted you in one broad sweep across heaven," Rainer Maria Rilke, *Rilke's Book of Hours*, translated by Anita Barrows and Joanna Macy, (New York: Riverhead, 2005), p. 83.

Day I: Afternoon

"Lord help us to gather our strength . . ." from Zbigniew Preisner, *Requiem for my friend*, Audio CD, Erato, 1999.

Day I: Twilight

"Bereavement is a universal"—C. S. Lewis, *A Grief Observed* (San Francisco: HarperCollins, 2001), p. 50.

"the earthly beloved"—C. S. Lewis, *A Grief Observed* (San Francisco: HarperCollins, 2001), pp. 66–67.

Day I: Close of the Day

In manus tuas—Roman Breviary, www.breviary.net/ordinary/ordincomp.htm.

Day I: Night

"Time is the canvas"—Rainer Maria Rilke, *Rilke's Book of Hours*, translated by Anita Barrows and Joanna Macy, (New York: Riverhead, 2005) p. 115.

"I am so deep inside it . . . makes me small"—Rainer Maria Rilke, *Rilke's Book of Hours*, translated by Anita Barrows and Joanna Macy, (New York: Riverhead, 2005) p. 191.

"The pain continues"—Ann Weems, "Lament Psalm Thirty," in *Psalms of Lament* (Louisville, KY: Westminster John Knox, 1995), p. 57.

"Remembered happiness is agony"—Donald Hall, "Midwinter Letter," in *Without: Poems* (Boston: Houghton Mifflin, 1998), p. 76.

"How much does matter matter?"—Mary Jo Bang, "Heartbreaking," in *Elegy: Poems by Mary Jo Bang* (Saint Paul, MN: Graywolf, 2007), p. 48.

Lamenting Virgin (*TheotokosThrenousa*), from diptych at the Monastery of the Tranfiguration, Meteora, Greece.

"Alone she saw"—George of Nikomedeia (ninth century), "Oratio in sepulturum Jesu Christi," *Patrologiae cursus completus, Series graeca,* J.-P. Migne (Paris, 1897–1904), vol. 100, p. 1489.

Lady of Vladimir, Tretyakov Gallery, Moscow, Russia.

Epitaphios [Lament] with Gold-thread Embroidery, Theodosia Poulopos (1599), Benaki Museum, Athens, Greece.

Day II: Dawn

"God speaks to each of us"—Rainer Maria Rilke, *Rilke's Book of Hours,* translated by Anita Barrows and Joanna Macy, (New York: Riverhead, 2005) , p. 119.

"This is another day"—*The Book of Common Prayer* (New York: Seabury, 1979), p. 461.

Day II: Daytime

"Ungiven gifts"—Ann Weems, "Lament Psalm Seven," in *Psalms of Lament* (Louisville, KY: Westminster John Knox, 1995), p. 12.

Day II: Noon

"What is left"—Mary Jo Bang, "The Role of Elegy," in *Elegy* (Saint Paul, MN: Graywolf, 2007), p.64.

"the dwelling-place of absence"—Donald Hall, "Midwinter Letter," in *Without: Poems* (Boston: Houghton Mifflin, 1998) p. 57.

Day II: Afternoon

"What do they celebrate"—Ann Weems, "Lament Psalm Nineteen," in *Psalms of Lament* (Louisville, KY: Westminster John Knox, 1995), p. 34.

Day II: Twilight

"Thought after thought"—C. S. Lewis, *A Grief Observed* (San Francisco: HarperCollins, 2001), p. 47.

Day II: Close of the Day

"O Christ, you wept when grief was raw"—John Bell, *The Last Journey: Songs for the Time of Grieving* (The Iona Community: Wild Goose Resource Group, 1996).

Day II: Night

"How could I not have saved you"—Mary Jo Bang, "Landscape with the Fall of Icarus," in *Elegy* (Saint Paul, MN: Graywolf, 2007), p. 24.

"Like water spilled on the ground"—2 Samuel 14:14 (NRSV).

"I weep for what was"—Ann Weems, "Lament Psalm Twenty-Nine," in *Psalms of Lament*, (Louisville, KY: Westminster John Knox, 1995), p. 55.

"The neverness of death"—this echoes Nicholas Wolterstorff, *Lament for a Son*, (Grand Rapids, MI: Eerdmans, 1987), p. 15.

Day III: Dawn

"Tell me you caught him"—Ann Weems, "Lament Psalm Twenty-Eight," in *Psalms of Lament*, (Louisville, KY: Westminster John Knox, 1995), pp. 52–53.

Day III: Mid-Morning

Wheatfield with a Reaper, Vincent van Gogh, Van Gogh Museum, Amsterdam, Netherlands.

Day III: Twilight

"So many are alive"—Rainer Maria Rilke, *Rilke's Book of Hours*, translated by Anita Barrows and Joanna Macy, (New York: Riverhead, 2005), p. 71.

"Can it be that there is no moon"—Online: http://allpoetry.com/Ariwara_no_Narihira (LV)" (freely rendered). Kenneth Rexroth translates the poem this way: "this is not the moon, / Nor is this the spring, / Of other springs, / And I alone/Am still the same." Rexroth, *One Hundred Poems from the Japanese*, p. 57.

"In the vacancy . . . revolve"—paraphrasing Mary Jo Bang, "We Took Our Places," in *Elegy*, (Saint Paul, MN: Graywolf, 2007), p. 6 ("In spite of its radical vacancy, the world continues to revolve").

Day III: Close of the Day

"Keep me as the apple of your eye"—"The Boisil Compline," in *Celtic Daily Prayer* (New York: HarperCollins, 2005), pp. 42–43.

Day III: Night

"Silver-toothed traps, their springs tightly wound and rust free" —paraphrasing May Jo Bang, "A Year Ends," in *Elegy* (Saint Paul, MN: Graywolf, 2007), p. 82 ("a silver-tooth trap,/The spring of which never rusted").

"The Homecoming of the Lost Son," Rembrandt van Rijn (1636), Rijksmuseum, Amsterdam, Netherlands.

Day IV: Twilight

"The Wounded Angel"—Hugo Simberg (1903), Ateneum Museum, Helsinki, Finland.

"She reconciled the ill-matched threads"—paraphrasing Rilke's Book of Hours, Rainer Maria Rilke, translated by Anita Barrows and Joanna Macy (New York: River head, 2005), p. 77.

"I shall accept my regrets"—Nicholas Wolterstorff, *Lament for a Son* (Grand Rapids, MI: Eerdmans, 1987), p. 65.

Day IV: Close of the Day

"I know in my heart"—Ann Weems, "Lament Psalm Seventeen," in *Psalms of Lament* (Louisville, KY: Westminster John Knox, 1995), p. 31.

Day IV: Night

"see things that dry-eyed [we] could not see,"—Nicholas Wolterstorff, *Lament for a Son* (Grand Rapids, MI: Eerdmans, 1987), p. 26.

"Passionate grief"—C. S. Lewis, *A Grief Observed* (San Francisco: HarperCollins, 2001), p. 54.

"as if the lifting"—C. S. Lewis, *A Grief Observed* (San Francisco: HarperCollins, 2001), p. 45.

"It is just at those moments"—C. S. Lewis, *A Grief Observed*, (San Francisco: HarperCollins, 2001), pp. 54–55.

Day V: Dawn

"My love, if I die and you don't,"—Pablo Neruda, Sonnet 92, in *One Hundred Sonnets*, translated by Stephen Tapscott (Austin: University of Texas Press, 1986), p. 195.

Day V: Twilight

"We don't really want grief,"—C. S. Lewis, *A Grief Observed* (San Francisco: HarperCollins, 2001), pp. 53–54.

Day V: Close of the Day

"Watch, now, dear Lord"—*Book of Common Prayer*, p. 134.

Day V: Night

"O God, why did you create a life"—Ann Weems, "Lament Psalm Seventeen," in *Psalms of Lament* (Louisville, KY: Westminster John Knox, 1995), p. 31.

"I'm slipping"—Rainer Maria Rilke, *Rilke'sBook of Hours*, translated by Anita Barrows and Joanna Macy (New York: Riverhead, 2005), p. 87.

Day VI: Dawn

"When I die"—Pablo Neruda, "Sonnet 89," in *One Hundred Sonnets*, translated by Stephen Tapscott (Austin: University of Texas Press, 1986), p. 189.

"If I die, survive me with such a pure force"—Pablo Neruda, "Sonnet 94," in *One Hundred Sonnets*, translated by Stephen Tapscott (Austin: University of Texas Press, 1986), p. 199.

Day VI: Midday

"Take him, earth, for cherishing," Prudentius, "The Burial of the Dead," translated by Helen Waddell, *Medieval Latin Lyrics* (Portland, OR: Four Courts, 2008), p. 45.

Magdalene Penitent, Donatello, Museo dell'Opera del Duomo, Florence, Italy.

Day VI: Twilight

Worn Out (also entitled, *At Eternity's Gate*), Vincent van Gogh, Van Gogh Museum, Amsterdam, Netherlands.

"The wall between us"—Rainer Maria Rilke, *Rilke's Books of Hours*, translated by Anita Barrows and Joanna Macy (New York: Riverhead, 2005), p. 53.

"Between the living world"—Wendell Berry, "The Cold Pane," in *A Part* (San Francisco: Northpoint, 1980), p. 8.

"the intersection of the timeless with time"—T. S. Eliot, "Dry Salvages," in *Four Quartets* (New York: Harcourt, Brace, Jovanovich, 1971), lines 201–2.

The luminous, haunted rose garden of "our first world"—T. S. Eliot, "Burnt Norton," in *Four Quartets* (New York: Harcourt, Brace, Jovanovich, 1971), line 21.

The dance at the "still point of the turning world"—T. S. Eliot, "Burnt Norton," in *Four Quartets* (New York: Harcourt, Brace, Jovanovich, 1971), line 62.

Time when "the kingfisher's wing . . . [answers] light to light"— T. S. Eliot, "Burnt Norton," in *Four Quartets* (New York: Harcourt, Brace, Jovanovich, 1971), lines 134–35.

"Communication of the dead . . . tongued with fire beyond the language of the living"—T. S. Eliot, "Little Gidding," in *Four Quartets* (New York: Harcourt, Brace, Jovanovich, 1971), lines 50–51.

"Midwinter spring," "suspended in time"—"springtime but not in time's covenant"—T. S. Eliot, "Little Gidding," in *Four Quartets* (New York: Harcourt, Brace, Jovanovich, 1971), lines 1, 3, 13–14.

Love, itself unmoving, causing movement, timeless "caught in the aspect of limitation"—Eliot, "Burnt Norton," in *Four Quartets* (New York: Harcourt, Brace, Jovanovich, 1971), line 167.

"To apprehend the point of intersection"—T.S. Eliot, "Dry Salvages," in Four Quartets (New York: Harcourt, Brace, Jovanovich, 1971), lines 204–6.

"Human kind cannot bear too much reality"—T. S. Eliot, "Burnt Norton," in *Four Quartets* (New York: Harcourt, Brace, Jovanovich, 1971), lines 42–43.

"enchainment of past and future"—T. S. Eliot, "Burnt Norton," in *Four Quartets* (New York: Harcourt, Brace, Jovanovich, 1971), lines 79–82.

Day VII: Daytime

The Holy Trinity, Andrei Rublev (ca. 1425–1427), Tretyakov Gallery, Moscow, Russia.

"God . . . allows us each of us to share"—Karl Barth, *Church Dogmatics*, III.2 (London: T&T Clark, 1960, 2004), p. 524.

Day VII: Twilight

"O God, why did you create a life/that includes death," Ann Weems, "Lament Psalm Seventeen," in *Psalms of Lament*, (Louisville, KY: Westminster John Knox, 1995), p. 31.

"Karl Barth offers a serious response . . ."—this discussion draws on Karl Barth, *Church Dogmatics*, III.2, 511–640.

Resurrection is a matter of life's completion, not its continuation—Karl Barth, *Dogmatics in Outline*, (New York: Harper & Row, 1959), p.154.

Day VII: Close of the Day

"One whose darkness is darker than night"—Rainer Maria Rilke, *Rilke's Book of Hours*, translated by Anita Barrows and Joanna Macy (New York: Riverhead, 2005), p. 145.

Day VII: Night

"The night is a huge house"—Rainer Maria Rilke, *Rilke's Book of Hours*, translated by Anita Barrows and Joanna Macy (New York: Riverhead, 2005), p. 145.

"O dark, dark, dark"—John Milton, *Samson Agonistes* (London: John Starkey, 1671), lines 80–82, 86–89.

"teeter on the brink"—Mary Jo Bang, "Enclosure," in *Elegy*, (Saint Paul, MN: Graywolf, 2007), p. 21.

"I shall never be a biped again"—C. S. Lewis, *A Grief Observed*, (San Francisco: HarperCollins, 2001), p. 53.

"Tonight all the hells of young grief have opened again"—C. S. Lewis, *A Grief Observed* (San Francisco: HarperCollins, 2001), pp. 56–57.

"The risen Christ kept his wounds"—paraphrasing Nicholas Wolterstorff, *Lament for a Son*, (Grand Rapids, MI: Eerdmans, 1987), pp. 92–93.

Day VII: Close of the Day II

"O Lord, my heart is not lifted up"—paraphrasing and adapting Psalm 131.

Day VIII: Twilight

"And all shall be well . . ."—Julian of Norwich (b. 1343), *Revelations of Divine Love*, (many editions—available at *Christian Classic Etherial Library,* http://www.ccel.org/ccel/julian/revelations.toc.html), ch. 27.

"I walked away . . ."—Lewis B. Smedes, *How Can It Be All Right When Everything Is All Wrong?* (Colorado Springs: WaterBrooks, 1999), pp.13–14, 16.

Day VIII: Close of the Day

"Come to me, O Comforter"—Ann Weems, "Lament Psalm Seven," in *Psalms of Lament*, (Louisville, KY: Westminster John Knox, 1995), p. 12.

Day IX: Mid-Morning

"It ceased to hurt me"—Emily Dickinson, *The Poems of Emily Dickinson*, edited by R. W. Franklin, (Cambridge, MA: Belknap, 1998), p. 466.

Day IX: Daytime

Peace Be Still, He Qi (2001), online: www.heqigallery.com.

Day IX: Twilight

"Instead of explaining our suffering God shares it"—Nicholas Wolterstorff, *Lament for a Son*, (Grand Rapids, MI: Eerdmans, 1987), p. 81.

Day IX: Close of the Day

"Calm me, O Lord, as You stilled the storm"—The Felgild Compline, *Celtic Daily Prayer: A Northumbrian Office* (New York: HarperCollins, 2005), p. 38.

Day IX: Night

"And all shall be well"—T. S. Eliot, "Little Giddings," in *Four Quartets* (New York: Harcourt, Brace, Jovanovich, 1971), lines 255–59.

Permissions

Mary Jo Bang, excerpts from "Heartbreaking," "The Role of Elegy," and "Enclosure" from *Elegy*. Copyright © 2007 by Mary Jo Bang. Reprinted with the permission of The Permissions Company, Inc., on behalf of Graywolf Press, www.graywolfpress.org.

Karl Barth, *Church Dogmatics* III.2 (London: T&T Clark International, 1960, 2004), p. 524. By kind permission of Continuum International Publishing Group.

"O Christ, You Wept" by J. L. Bell

"Since We Are Summoned" by J. L. Bell. Copyright © 1996, Wild Goose Resource Group, Iona Community, Scotland, GIA Publications, Inc., exclusive North American agent, 7404 S. Mason Ave., Chicago, IL 60638, www.giamusic.com 800.442.1358. All rights reserved. Used by permission.

Wendell Berry, "The Cold Pane," in *A Part* (Berkeley, CA: Counterpoint Press). Used by permission.

"The Ebba Compline," "The Boisil Compline," and "The Felgild Compline." *Celtic Daily Prayers*. Published with the kind permission of the Northumbria Community Trust.

Emily Dickinson, "It ceased to hurt me, though so slow" (J 584 / F 421). Reprinted by permission of the publishers and the Trustees of Amherst College from *The Poems of Emily Dickinson: Variorum Edition*, edited by Ralph W. Franklin, Cambridge, MA: The Belknap Press of Harvard University Press, Copyright © 1998 by the President and Fellows of Harvard College. Copyright © 1951, 1955, 1979, 1983 by the President and Fellows of Harvard College.

Donatello, *Magdalene Penitent*, ca. 1453–1455, Museo dell'Opera del Duomo, Florence, IT. Used by permission.

T. S. Eliot's *Four Quartets* is used by permission of publishers Faber and Faber Ltd for permission throughout Canada.

Theodosia Poulopo, *Epitaphios with Gold-thread Embroidery*, 1599, Benaki Museum, Athens, Greece. Used by permission.

Excerpts from "Midsummer Letter" and "Midwinter Letter" from *Without: Poems* by Donald Hall. Copyright © 1998 by Donald Hall. Reprinted by permission of Houghton Mifflin Harcourt Publishing Company. All rights reserved.

The Lamenting Virgin (*Theotokos Threnousa*), from diptych, Monastery of the Transfiguration, Meteora, Greece. Used by permission.

A Grief Observed by C. S. Lewis, copyright © C. S. Lewis Pte. Ltd. 1961. Extract reprinted by permission.

From 100 *Love Sonnets: Cien sonetos de amor* by Pablo Neruda, translated by Stephen Tapscott, Copyright © Pablo Neruda 1959 and Fundacion Pablo Neruda, Copyright © 1986 by the University of Texas Press. By permission of the University of Texas Press.

Prudentius, "The Burial of the Dead" from Helen Waddell, *Mediaeval Latin Lyrics* (Portland, OR: Four Courts Press, 2008). Used by permission of Four Courts Press.

"Peace Be Still" by Dr. He Qi (www.heqigallery.com) is used by permission.

Rembrandt van Rijn, *The Return of the Lost Son (De thuiskomst van de verloren zoon)*, 1636, Rijks Museum, Amsterdam, NL. Used by permission.

"Ariwara no Narihira (LV)" and "Narihira (LVI)." By Kenneth Rexroth, from *One Hundred Poems from the Japanese, copyright* ©1955 by New Directions Publishing Corp. Reprinted by permission of New Directions Publishing Corp.

From *Rilke's Book of Hours: Love Poems to God* by Rainer Maria Rilke, translated by Anita Barrows and Joanna Macy, copyright © 1996 by Anita Barrows and Joanna Macy. Used by permission of Riverhead Books, an imprint of Penguin Group (USA) Inc.

Rainer Maria Rilke, "Requiem for a Friend," from *The Selected Poetry of Rainer Maria Rilke*, trans. Stephen Mitchell (New York: Random House, 1982). Used by permission.

The images of Andrei Rublev's *Holy Trinity* and the unknown icon painter's *Our Lady of Vladimir* are the copyrighted property of The State Tretyakov Gallery in Moscow, Russia, and are used by permission.

Hugo Simberg, *Wounded Angel*, 1903, Ateneum Museum, Helsinki, FI. Photographed by Hannu Aaltonen of the Central Art Archives of the Finnish National Gallery. Used by permission.

From *How Can It Be All Right When Everything Is All Wrong?* By Lewis B. Smedes, copyright © E1982, 1999 by Lewis B. Smedes. Used by permission of WaterBrook Multnomah, an imprint of the Crown Publishing Group, a division of Random House, Inc.

Vincent van Gogh (1853–1890)

Worn Out, 1882

Van Gogh Museum, Amsterdam (Vincent van Gogh Foundation)/Van Gogh Museum, Amsterdam (Vincent van Gogh Foundation) d378V/1962. Used by permission.

Vincent van Gogh (1853–1890)

Permissions

Wheatfield With a Reaper, 1889

Van Gogh Museum, Amsterdam (Vincent van Gogh Foundation)/Van Gogh Museum, Amsterdam (Vincent van Gogh Foundation) s49V/1962. Used by permission.

From *Psalms of Lament*. © 1995 Ann Barr Weems. Used by permission of Westminster John Knox Press. www.wjkbooks.com.

From Nicholas Wolterstorff's *Lament for a Son* (Grand Rapids, MI: Eerdmans, 1987). Reprinted by permission of the publisher; all rights reserved.